Detoxify Your Way to Health and Happiness

Detoxify Your Way to Health and Happiness

TANUSHREE PODDER

Viva Books

New Delhi | Mumbai | Chennai | Kolkata | Bangalore | Hyderabad | Kochi

First Published 2006
Reprint 2008

VIVA BOOKS PRIVATE LIMITED

4737/23 Ansari Road, Daryaganj, New Delhi 110 002
E-mail: vivadelhi@vivagroupindia.net, Tel. 42242200

Plot No. 76, Service Industries, Shirvane, Sector 1, Nerul, Navi Mumbai 400 706
E-mail: vivamumbai@vivagroupindia.net, Tel. 27721273, 27721274

Jamals Fazal Chambers, 26 Greams Road, Chennai 600 006
E-mail: vivachennai@vivagroupindia.net, Tel. 28290304, 28294241

B-103, Jindal Towers, 21/1A/3 Darga Road, Kolkata 700 017
E-mail: vivakolkata@vivagroupindia.net, Tel. 22836381, 22816713

7, Sovereign Park Apartments, 56-58, K. R. Road, Basavanagudi, Bangalore 560 004
E-mail: vivabangalore@vivagroupindia.net, Tel. 26607409, 26607410

101-102 Mughal Marc Apartments, 3-4-637 to 641, Narayanguda, Hyderabad 500 029
E-mail: vivahyderabad@vivagroupindia.net, Tel. 27564481, 27564482

Beevi Towers, First Floor, SRM Road, Kaloor, Kochi 682 018, Kerala
E-mail: vivakochi@vivagroupindia.net, Tel: 0484-2403055, 2403056

www.vivagroupindia.com

ISBN-10: 81-309-0272-9
ISBN-13: 978-81-309-0272-2

Published by Vinod Vasishtha for Viva Books Private Limited,
4737/23, Ansari Road, New Delhi-110 002.

Printed and bound by Raj Press, R-3, Inderpuri, New Delhi - 110012

Dedication

For my daughters, Anupriya and Ankita

Contents

SECTION III

SECTION IV

SECTION V

SECTION VI

SECTION VII

Acknowledgements

The birth of each book involves the dedication of many people. From the person who acts as the sounding board to the editor who shares the pangs of the birth as intensely as the author, each one is equally indispensable.

As usual, my husband has been the sounding board with whom I had many disagreements as we discussed the contents that needed to fit into the hundred odd pages of the manuscript. His patience is commendable.

This book couldn't have adorned the book shelves without the great work put in by my editor.

Prologue

With newer and deadlier diseases making an appearance it was natural that researchers and the medical fraternity should look into the causes of their proliferation. In the last half-century, the findings of most of these researches pointed to a single word – 'toxin'.

Toxins are known to cause diseases like cancer. They also cause premature ageing and depression. Toxins are the greatest foes of mankind. Be it toxic thoughts, environment or food, we have a surfeit of them all around us. The word toxin is described as poison, contaminant and pollution in the lexicon. Today, almost every disease on this planet can be traced back to the toxins that surround us.

Although toxins have always been present in some form or the other, in the recent years there has been a sharp growth in the toxicity-related diseases, some of them almost incurable. Arthritis, allergies, obesity, cancer and cardiovascular disease and many skin problems are just a few of the bodily ailments that occur due to the wide range of toxins in and around us. In addition, a wide range of symptoms, such as headaches, fatigue, pains, coughs, gastrointestinal problems, and problems from immune weakness, can all be related to toxicity.

Toxic elements are not just found in our food, environment and water, they exist in the form of highly dangerous emotions and thoughts in our minds, too. Toxic emotions and thoughts are as harmful to our body as the toxic food and water. Many of the psychosomatic diseases have their origin in the negative emotions that rule our mind.

A regular process of detoxifying prevents degeneration and helps in rejuvenating the body. On the physical level, it can help clear congestions, illnesses, and disease potential. It can recharge and refresh as well as raise the energy level in the body. On the mental plane detoxification cleanses the mind of negative thoughts. Emotionally, detoxification helps us release and express feelings, especially hidden frustrations, anger, resentments, or fear, which are quite detrimental to the well being of a person. It also replaces these emotions with the positive ones of forgiveness, love, joy, and hope. On a spiritual level, it gifts us with clarity of self and an enhancement of the purpose of life. Detoxifying can change the way we feel about ourselves as well as the others around us. It can totally transform our lives.

The idea of writing this book occurred when a close friend was diagnosed with cancer. Her suffering led me to research into the factors that could be called carcinogenic. And what I unearthed was a shocking revelation about the dangers that lurk in modern lifestyle and environment. Despite chemotherapy and other forms of treatment when my friend succumbed to the disease, I realised it was time to pen the facts about toxins and bring to light the benefits associated with detoxification. While detoxification will not cure cancer, it can definitely help in preventing it.

Tanushree Podder

SECTION I

1

DETOXIFICATION

You spring-clean your house, wash your car periodically and subject almost every gadget you own to regular servicing. In fact, most of your gadgets and equipments must be under the ubiquitous AMC (Annual Maintenance Contract). Just as grime gradually builds up in our homes over months, toxins build up in our bodies. Yet, not many of us do anything to service or clean the body, mind and soul of the accumulated garbage. Don't forget that unlike the gadgets most of the body parts are irreplaceable. There are no spare parts available for them. Throughout our life we continuously heap all kinds of abuse on our body. Wrong food, wrong lifestyle, wrong thoughts, wrong breathing, wrong habits – in short, almost every kind of wrong that is possible is loaded on it.

Finally, when the abuse reaches the saturation point, our body begins to protest, and the protest comes in the form of varied diseases and discomforts. We immediately make a beeline for a doctor expecting miraculous healing for our ailments, least realising that a regular detoxification programme would have prevented the disease.

Our body has a team of efficient cleaners that do their work diligently and incessantly. They ensure that the processes of bacteria elimination, virus eradication and toxin purging carry on continuously so that we can remain healthy and smiling. Like an ultra-modern superhighway the circulatory system carries endless load of blood vessels throughout the body without mishap till we deposit roadblocks on it, in the form of cholesterol. Likewise, the liver filters about eighty-six litres of blood every hour, clearing all toxins from it. But when an overload of toxins hits our system, we can't expect it to cope with the deadly stuff. Just as the most efficient machinery can break down at times, the cleaning mechanisms of the body also slow down at times when we subject ourselves to excesses.

Toxins are the greatest foes of mankind. Toxicity is of much greater concern in this century than ever before. There are many new chemicals in the air and water leading to severe pollution. The number of lethal pesticides being used by the farmers to increase produce could cover a small notebook. The preservatives and colorants used by the food industry are a hazard that we are blissfully unaware of. The bright yellow jalebis, the delicious red curries and the delectable kebabs with heightened colours are happily consumed by people in their favourite restaurants. Many of the colours used to make the food attractive are carcinogenic in nature. If it were not for the recent controversy about the use of Sudan I, a dangerous colorant in red chillies exported to UK, many of us would have remained quite ignorant about the dangers of these adulterants.

The high level of pesticide in soft drinks and the presence of maggots in chocolates created a stir some time back, but it was quickly forgotten, and most people went back to the products without hesitation within a span of weeks. Some had not even abstained from consuming them during the height of controversy. The choice is clearly ours – to remain healthy or to give in to the demands of the taste buds.

We ingest new chemicals, use more drugs of all kinds, eat adulterated and refined foods and abuse ourselves with various stimulants and sedatives on a daily basis. Even innocuous-seeming things like household cleaners, solvents, cigarette smoke and air fresheners contribute to a toxic environment. Then, there are the automobile exhaust fumes, smoggy air, industrial fumes, and pesticides and other agricultural chemicals that can be quite lethal for the human species. We are constantly wading our way through all kinds of lethal garbage exposing ourselves to various toxins.

Why? The very soaps and detergents that you use to clean your dishes and clothes may have toxic effect if there are residual chemicals after the wash. Often, you might have noticed a white layer of powdery substance after the utensils have been washed and dried. The coils, mats and vapour we use at home to drive away insects and mosquitoes may have a lethal effect on them, but our bodies suffer some mild effects, too. Who knows how the chemicals may affect us over a period of time? As the insects develop immunity and the strength of chemicals is raised to retain their efficacy, human beings will be exposed to more potent chemicals. The very clothes you wear could contain toxic dyes. The food you order for home delivery from a local eatery could come wrapped in plastic that may not be of food-grade quality. The packaged food that you buy off the shelves contains several preservatives and chemicals that may cause harm. Hundreds of such toxins lurk around our homes without causing any suspicion or concern.

Are you aware that the mercury content in your dental fillings also causes toxic effects? A typical amalgam filling contains mercury. Researchers say that every time the filling is exposed to pressure from chewing, mercury vapours are released in the body, resulting in the accumulation of the heavy metal in the liver and other organs.

Here we are simply talking about the toxins that come from outside, but what about the toxins we generate inside our bodies through toxic thoughts, stress, negative emotions and anxiety? Over a period of time, the accumulated effect of these can be as harmful as those of the external toxins. The most important thing is that the external toxins are mostly beyond our control but the internal ones can be easily controlled. Stress, negative emotions and toxic thoughts can be overpowered by a little determination and effort.

A body overloaded with toxins suffers from various ailments ranging from the mild to the complicated. Constipation, bloated stomach, gas, fatigue, mental weakness, headaches, poor skin, poor memory, depression, body odour and bad breath are just some of the problems caused by toxicity.

Now you are worried! If it is as dire as it sounds, how does one get rid of the toxins? The process of getting rid of these deadly elements is known as detoxification, detox, in short. Detoxification, however, cannot work in isolation. It has to combine with judicious food habits, regular exercise and a spiritual outlook. Besides, detoxifying the body once in a lifetime and then forgetting about it doesn't work. Maintenance of good physical condition would involve making a series of lifestyle changes with a holistic approach towards health and well-being.

What is detoxification?

Our bodies perform detoxification relentlessly and naturally, every day. Detoxification is a normal body process of eliminating or neutralising toxins through the colon, liver, kidneys, lungs, lymph and skin. In fact, the process of internal detoxification is one of our body's basic automatic functions. The circulatory and lymphatic system, along with the colon, urino-genital system and the liver, works systematically to cleanse out the junk from the body. Just as our hearts beat non-stop and our lungs breathe continuously, our metabolic processes incessantly dispose accumulated toxic matter from the body.

Then why should you bother?

Well, it would be an ideal situation if the bodily systems could handle all the toxins as nature intended them to do. But the world today is laden with more pollutants and external toxins than the body can handle. The body systems and organs that were once capable of cleaning out unwanted substances are now completely overloaded. Despite their best effort, many unwanted substances continue to remain in our tissues. Ideally, we should live in a pollution-free environment, eat untainted foods and drink pure water. We know this isn't possible, so the next best thing is to keep pollutants to a minimum and to periodically get rid of them through a detoxification programme.

So what should you do?

It is quite simple, really. If our bodies can't handle the load of toxins, we have to help them in their task by undertaking regular detoxification just as we spring-clean our homes. To undertake the task, we have to fight against all kinds of toxins – the ones that come through food, water, air and thoughts, in fact, through every possible route, to invade our bodies. Detoxification through special cleansing diets may greatly reduce diseases, especially diseases like cancer, arthritis and diabetes. Our unhealthy diet with too much animal protein, too much fat, too much caffeine and alcohol radically alters our internal ecosystems. A good cleansing programme can restore body vitality against environmental toxins that pave the way for disease-bearing bacteria, viruses and parasites.

Detoxification is a process that has been used for a long time by doctors and clinics to recover alcoholics and drug addicts. Today, it has become a necessity for every individual if he wants to avoid disease. Everyone can benefit from a once- or twice-a-year mild 'spring cleaning' for general health maintenance. Detoxification involves dietary and lifestyle changes that reduce intake of toxins and improve elimination. Avoiding chemicals that come to our body from food or other sources, refined food, sugar, caffeine, alcohol and tobacco helps minimise the toxin load. Drinking lots of pure water and increasing fibre by including more fruits and vegetables in the diet are important to achive the detoxification goal.

Detoxification is not just required for the purpose of avoiding disease. It has an overall beneficial impact on our body, mind and soul. It leads to rejuvenation, retards ageing, clears skin, improves flexibility and brings about greater efficiency of the senses, boundless energy and improved performance in all areas of life. It also makes a person more relaxed, creative and spiritual. Weight loss and improved fertility are an added bonus.

A detox programme aims to remove the cause of disease before it makes us ill. It's a time-honoured way to keep immune response high, elimination regular, circulation sound, and stress under control, so that your body can handle the toxicity it encounters. A regular detox programme two or three times a year makes a big difference not only to the health but also to the quality of life.

Why should you detoxify?

Would you ever drive an expensive car with its carburettor choked and its fuel tank floating with muck? No, of course, you won't!

Then why should you go around with a body that is chock-full with toxins? It is akin to walking around with a time bomb ticking inside your belly.

Our exposure to pollutants is beyond the scale that can be handled by our immune system. Industrial chemicals, pollutants in our water, pesticides, additives in our foods, heavy metals and residues from drugs are affecting the human body in increasingly severe forms. Right from tissue damage to sensory deterioration, these toxins affect every system of the body. Certain pesticides and pollutants are linked to birth defects, hormone problems, psychological disorders and breast cancer. Yet, ignorant farmers continue to use these for better yield. Cows are injected with toxic hormonal injections for better milk production.

Food preservatives, additives, colours, in fact, all that goes into most products on the supermarket shelves, are increasingly consumed by people without a thought to the toxic effect of these elements on the body. At least, these are within our control. What about those that lie beyond our control?

Some of the chemicals are so common that we are not even aware of the harm they cause to our body. For instance, the asbestos water pipes or corroded pipes that carry water to our homes are not even given a thought. Excess chlorine or fluoride in water can cause damage to body cells; the mercury filling that you have in your tooth may not bother you for a long time although the damage may occur in a silent manner. The ill effects connected with these elements work their way into our bodies faster than imagined, causing allergies and ailments.

To the millions of synthetic substances that are recorded, a colossal number of new ones are added each year. According to a recent study, no less than 25,000 synthetic elements are added to the list each year. Thousands of these are manufactured commercially. I am not even including things like caffeine, alcohol, exhaust fumes and tobacco smoke in the list of toxins, although we are exposed to them every day. Of the thousands of chemicals and elements introduced in the world each year, no more than a few hundred are tested for toxicity. The situation is much worse in the developing countries where no viable safeguards are in place.

We also import a lot of garbage from the developed countries in the name of industrialisation and growth. It is a known fact that toxic wastes have been dumped into our country by developed countries. These arrive in India through the collusion of unprincipled politicians, unscrupulous dealers and corrupt officials.

Scary, isn't it? Some of these chemicals have been found to be carcinogenic in nature and may even cause genetic alteration on prolonged exposure. World Health Organisation research links environmental chemicals to most kinds of cancers.

As the body is faced with increasing number of toxic matter beyond the handling capacity of our immune system, we begin to suffer from various ailments. But, some of the harmful effects can definitely be controlled through regular cleansing and detoxification. The least we can do is to take preventive measures in order to keep our own systems in healthy condition so that toxins are eliminated quickly.

Here are some simple questions you could ask yourself.

Do you feel sluggish and jaded, like you need a good spring-cleaning?
Do you feel your system clogged with the wrong kinds of food?
Do you often feel blue and depressed?
Do you feel the need to streamline your body processes for more energy?
Do you want to prevent disease?
Do you feel the need to rejuvenate your body?
Do you feel that your steps lack a spring?
Do you want to clear up your skin?
Do you want to slow ageing and improve body flexibility?

If the answer to most questions is 'yes', you need to begin your detoxification programme right away.

What needs to be done?

We are all aware that unhealthy levels of stress and negative emotions can work as poisons. We can try and reduce or control the stress levels. The fast pace of life has given birth to a whole new lifestyle that is not just unhealthy but dangerous. The ready-made, off-the-shelf kind of foods which come in attractive and convenient packages, highly advertised by the companies, are just the stuff that can cause disease. The highly-processed food diet born out of extremely busy life is also severely unbalanced and overburdens the elimination system. Lack of exercise contributes to toxicity too. The body's natural cleansing cycle of oxygen and vital nutrients depends upon exercise. A stagnant system encourages toxic build-up. These are things that can be altered with a little effort.

When you consider the difference a little effort and discipline can make to your health factor, you would not hesitate for a moment to make that effort. Arthritis, allergies, obesity, cancer, cardiovascular disease and many skin problems are just a few of the bodily ailments that occur due to the wide range of toxins in and around us. Ailments like headaches, fatigue, pains, coughs and gastrointestinal problems find their roots in the high degree of toxic elements in and around us.

Backaches, frequent colds, irritated eyes, immune-weakness, sinus congestion, fever, sleepiness, insomnia, dizziness, mood changes, anxiety, depression, fatigue, skin rashes, hives, nausea, indigestion, anorexia, bad breath, constipation, tight or stiff neck, headaches, sore throat, wheezing, joint pains, and cough – if you suffer from any or many of these ailments, a detoxification programme will definitely alleviate your problems.

RECAP

Just as grime gradually builds up in our homes over months, toxins build up in our bodies.

- ➥ The word toxin is described as poison, contaminant and pollution in the lexicon. Toxins can cause cancer. They can also cause premature ageing and decay our souls.
- ➥ We are constantly wading our way through all kinds of lethal garbage, exposing ourselves to various toxins.
- ➥ Arthritis, allergies, obesity, cancer and cardiovascular disease, and many skin problems occur due to toxins around us.
- ➥ Backaches, frequent colds, irritated eyes, immune-weakness, sinus congestion, fever, sleepiness,

▶▶

insomnia, dizziness, mood changes, anxiety, depression and fatigue are all toxin-related problems.

- Skin rashes, hives, nausea, indigestion, anorexia, bad breath, constipation, tight or stiff neck, headaches, sore throat, wheezing, joint pains, and cough – if you suffer from any or many of these ailments, a detoxification programme will definitely alleviate your problems.

2

THE DEADLY TOXINS

Toxicity occurs in our body when we take in more than we can utilise and eliminate. Homeostasis means that our body functions are in balance. This balance is disturbed when we feed ourselves more than we can utilise or partake of specific substances that are toxic. Toxicity may depend on the dosage, frequency or potency of the toxin. A toxin may produce an immediate or rapid onset of symptoms, as many pesticides and some drugs do; possibly, even more commonly, it may cause some long-term negative effect.

What is more dangerous is that toxins can cause harmful effects on generations of people. In a recent study, researchers in the US found that toxic chemicals that were ingested by grandparents could harm several generations. The findings, published in the journal *Science*, suggest that toxins may play a role in inherited diseases now blamed on genetic mutations. For instance, if your grandparents suffered from the toxins contained in DDT, the harmful toxins could have adverse effects on your health. The researchers found that the transmitted toxins could cause health damages up to four generations.

Air pollution is taking its toll on the younger generation by manifesting in respiratory ailments. According to a leading Mumbai pathologist, there is a significant increase in the cases of respiratory disorders in children in the last one decade. Among the pollutants carbon monoxide is the principal culprit. When it combines with dust and moisture and becomes smog, it is even more lethal. Inhaling the smog or air laden with carbon monoxide affects a child's immune system, rendering him an easy prey for several diseases. Pollution first affects the lungs. A gamut of allergens are inhaled along with the pollutants, which turn the healthy pink lungs into dark black ones, causing respiratory problems like asthma, bronchitis, chronic colds, sneezing, recurrent pneumonia and tuberculosis. In fact, an increase in the cases of tuberculosis is causing serious concerns to the doctors.

By now you have got a fair idea about what toxins can do to our health. Toxins are lethal and there is no doubt about that fact. Our body also generates toxins through its normal everyday functions. Biochemical, cellular and bodily activities produce substances that need to be eliminated. A sluggish system does not eliminate these toxic matters efficiently, and this can cause several diseases. Negative thoughts and emotions as well as stress generate increased biochemical toxicity. Elimination of these toxins is essential to the well-being and good health of the body and mind.

Toxins are mainly of two types – the exogenous and the endogenous. Exogenous toxins are those molecular structures that enter the body from the environment, for which the body has no use and which may also cause damage. Endogenous toxins are products of metabolism of which the body must rid itself.

Exogenous toxins are primarily products of the petrochemical and industrial ages. Industry has brought with it high exposure to toxic heavy metals, namely aluminium, antimony, arsenic, beryllium, bismuth, cadmium, lead, mercury, nickel, platinum, silver, thallium, thorium, tin and uranium. In the pre-industrial age man had almost no exposure to these elements except perhaps silver and lead. In our evolution the exposure has been so meagre that human biochemistry has made no use of these metals. Therefore, when these metals enter the human body, the only thing they can do is to replace the nutritional metals (such as manganese, magnesium, etc.) in enzyme systems. They depress the function of the enzymes and cause immense imbalance in the system.

Before we throw up our hands and complain about the environmental toxic material, let us not forget that we are a part of the system where we also do our bit in adding to the nuisance. The plastic bags, fuel emissions, unhygienic public behaviour, all add to the growing pollution in the environment. We do not protect the trees around us, neither make efforts to rise in protest against the wrong governmental decisions undertaken to denude the land of forests. Collective forces can wreak havoc on the sinister designs of the vested interests of land mafia, timber mafia and wildlife poachers. Each of us can contribute to the wellness of the environment by doing our bit as the citizens of the earth. We owe it to our children to leave behind a legacy of greenery and health.

Most of us would rather carry a plastic carry bag than one made of cloth, and dump our garbage in the nearest spot without a thought to the environment. We don't hesitate to leave behind plastic and garbage after a picnic in a beautiful forested area or a day on the beach. Many of us do not bother to keep in check the pollutants that are discharged by our vehicles. All we do is to complain about the growing pollution around us without finding ways to reduce the menace.

While your contribution to the removal of external toxic matter may remain a token effort, there is much you can do to control the internal toxins.

Internal detoxification is the process of clearing toxins from the body and clearing excess mucus and body blocks. An astounding five litres of blood is circulated through the body every minute carrying with it the wastes as well as the nutrition for the cells. Inadequate elimination of the toxins through our kidneys, respiratory tract and skin add to increased levels of toxins in the body. Certain problems like poor digestion, colon and liver sluggishness impair the ability of the body to get rid of the toxins.

Through detoxification, we clear and filter toxins and waste and allow our body to work on enhancing its basic functions. Our body handles toxins by neutralising, transforming or eliminating them. For example, many antioxidant nutrients may neutralise free-radical molecules. The liver helps transform many toxic substances into harmless agents, while the blood carries wastes to the kidneys; the liver also dumps wastes through the bile into the intestines, where much waste is eliminated. We also clear toxins through sweating, from exercise or heat. Our sinuses and skin may also be accessory elimination organs whereby excess mucus or toxins can be released, as with sinus congestion or skin rashes respectively.

Detoxification involves dietary and lifestyle changes that reduce intake of toxins and improve elimination. The first step to the detoxification process is to avoid chemicals from food or other sources, refined food, sugar, caffeine, alcohol and tobacco. Increasing the intake of fruits and vegetables in the diet and drinking enough water are equally important.

RECAP

- Toxins are mainly of two types – the exogenous and the endogenous.
- Exogenous toxins are those molecular structures that enter the body from the environment, for which the body has no use and which may also cause damage.
- Endogenous toxins are products of metabolism, of which the body must rid itself. Symptoms such as headaches, fatigue, pains, coughs, gastrointestinal problems and problems from immune weakness can all be related to toxicity.
- Stronger chemicals, air and water pollution, radiation and nuclear power, even innocuous-seeming things like household cleaners, solvents, cigarette smoke and air fresheners contribute to a toxic environment.
- Automobile exhaust fumes, smoggy air, industrial fumes, and pesticides and other agricultural chemicals add to the toxic effect.
- A detoxification programme aims to remove the cause of disease before it makes us ill.
- Its aim is to keep immune response high, elimination regular, circulation efficient, and stress levels under control.

3

DETOXIFYING THE BODY

Have you ever driven your car with a foot on the brake or with some dirt in the fuel tank? The car sputters and stalls. It doesn't run smoothly. So what do you do?

You remove your foot from the brake or clean up the fuel tank. Using the same analogy, where your body is like the car, can you imagine what would happen if some dirt clogged the systems. The body would stall, and you would feel fatigued. Detoxification of the body is like the cleaning up of the fuel tank of your car. The aim is to rest our overloaded digestive organs, liver, gall bladder and kidneys and allow them to rejuvenate. Can you imagine any machinery in the world running non-stop without maintenance? Not even the most efficient and outstanding machine would be able to do so.

Then why should your body run without maintenance?

Of course, it doesn't. It is a fallacy to believe that we will live without making any effort towards attaining good health. Walking into the sunset with glowing faces, as shown in the movies, can only occur when one takes adequate care of the body as well as the mind. Like everything else, health, happiness and wellness need to be worked upon. We achieve a state of homeostasis when all our body functions are in balance. Homeostasis is the process by which our body sustains continuity of internal conditions. The body goes through complex metabolic processes and produces potentially toxic waste products. It also uses up precious elements that need to be constantly restored. The balance between the elements is accomplished through homeostasis.

This balance is disturbed when we overeat or eat substances that can generate toxins. Of course, if our body is working well, with good immune and eliminative functions, we can handle our basic everyday exposure to toxins. Toxicity occurs in our body when we take in more than we can utilise and eliminate. A toxin may produce an immediate start of symptoms, as seen in the case of many pesticides and drugs. It could also cause some long-term negative effect, as in the case of asbestos exposure leading to lung cancer.

After a detox programme, the body starts rebalancing, energy levels rise physically, psychologically and sexually, and creativity begins to expand. You start feeling like a different person, rejuvenated and refreshed. Your outlook and attitude change; you feel totally energised.

An inefficient digestive system can impair memory and mental clarity. It can lead to a bloated and distended stomach, gas, headache, sluggishness and fatigue. Similarly, a respiratory system that doesn't do its job can lead to wheezing, breathlessness and lack of mental clarity. Whether it is the excretory, reproductive, respiratory, nervous, circulatory and digestive system, or any other system, their peak working conditions have to be maintained for a healthy existence.

Traditional detox regimens range from the mild and pleasurable ones like saunas, massages and body brushing to the unpleasant ones like fasting, colonic irrigation and bowel enemas. Making simple dietary changes is the safest and perhaps most effective way to detox.

What are the systems that can be easily detoxified?

Digestive

Respiratory

Excretory

Skin

Detoxification achieves:

A clean and healthy digestive tract without any trace of toxins, waste matter and harmful bacteria.

The cleansing effect carries itself to the liver, kidneys and circulatory system.

Stimulated and strengthened immune system.

The mind becomes clearer and the brain works better.

The skin glows.

Harmful food habits are reversed.

The added bonus is significant weight loss and a feeling of well-being.

RECAP

- Homeostasis is the process by which our body sustains continuity of internal conditions.
- This balance is disturbed when we overeat or eat substances that can generate toxins.
- Toxicity occurs in our body when we take in more than we can utilise and eliminate. A toxin may

produce an immediate start of symptoms, as seen in the case of many pesticides and drugs.

- It could also cause some long-term negative effect, as in the case of asbestos-exposure leading to lung cancer.
- An inefficient digestive system can impair memory and mental clarity. It can lead to a bloated and distended stomach, gas, headache, sluggishness and fatigue.
- A respiratory system that doesn't do its job can lead to wheezing, breathlessness and lack of mental clarity.

4

DETOXIFYING THE DIGESTIVE SYSTEM

The digestive system is a complex system made up of many organs and hormones. To clean the accumulated waste from the digestive tract requires effort. Imagine, if you kept pouring foodstuff, raw and cooked, into your drain, through the day, what would happen? Unless it is drained out, the entire lot would begin putrefying inside, leaving bad smell and bacteria. It would become impossible to remain in the vicinity of such a drain. Now think of the digestive system. Throughout the day we keep pouring all kinds of food and drinks in it. If these were not properly eliminated, the resultant mess would be something like the garbage in the drain. Can you visualise what a dirty, clogged-up digestive tract can look like? Much like a clogged drain, I think. Smelly, dirty and offensive! The very thought seems repulsive, doesn't it? So, why not begin to unclog and clear the mess?

A clogged digestive system does a lot of harm. It extracts its revenge by throwing up problems like pimples, arthritis, allergies and offensive breath, apart from the directly linked ailments like gas, stomachache, heartburn, constipation, etc. You feel perennially tired and run down. At the same time, it is not very difficult to get the digestion process working efficiently.

In today's fast-paced life, it is a series of deadlines, unhealthy stress levels, and hastily-gobbled meals for most of us. We add more junk to our system than we can really deal with. The problem this results in, is excessive fat intake, which leads to the formation of free radicals that can trigger off faster ageing. Illnesses and stress-related ailments are also caused by such unhealthy eating habits, and before you realise it, your trips to the doctor get a little more frequent than before.

So what must you do to detoxify your system? It simply means going in for a healthier eating pattern with fewer toxic substances in it. Detoxification involves resting, cleaning and nourishing the body inside out. By removing and eliminating toxins and then feeding your body with healthy nutrients, detoxifying can help protect you from disease and renew your ability to maintain optimum health.

It is difficult to escape the lure of tongue-tickling food and consume the food that is insipid and lacks the tang and tingle of various spices and fat. Food that is not pleasing to our palate rarely finds its way to the dining table. Not many of us would like to eat steamed vegetables or salads if we have the option of gorging on butter chicken and biryani. Nor do we want to trouble our minds with counting calories or balancing them. It is so much more comfortable and hassle-free to let the tongue dictate its terms. In any case, most of us learn to live with the little discomforts caused by unwise eating. Few care for the little nagging pains or gastric problems that occur as warning signs from time to time. It is only when the little discomforts take on giant proportions that we rush to doctors, specialists and dieticians to seek the panacea that will bring relief to our body. First, we spend our hard-earned money to buy the discomfort and then spend loads of it on doctors and medicines to cure the discomfort.

The body must be given the right fuel. Just as using diesel for a petrol vehicle will damage it, so will the wrong fuel for our body spoil it. The realisation that the right kind of food could ward off most of the diseases and keep the heart ticking comfortably for a long time is slowly dawning on the human race. Food is the single most important factor besides exercise that can keep the body supple, active and healthy. All these things are proven medical facts, but human nature is such that it heeds to the warning signals only when things have gone too far. Obesity is one of the biggest problems facing the health experts and most of the diseases find their roots in this problem. Even as the medical fraternity is struggling to combat the rising cases of obesity, more and more people are joining the ranks of obese population.

Some of the harmful foods that we don't seem to be able to live without are sugar, salt, caffeine, red meat and other animal proteins, refined flour and saturated fats. In order to detoxify your digestive system it is essential to cut down these elements and introduce healthy options. Preservatives and food additives are something you should watch out for. The biggest culprits among food additives are hydrogenated oil and high-fructose corn syrup. These two are the most harmful ingredients to look for on food labels.

Detoxification is a relative term. Anything that supports our elimination can be said to help us detoxify. Doing nothing more than drinking an extra litre of water a day will usually help us eliminate more toxins. Eating more fruits and vegetables like the high-water-content-cleansing foods, and less meat and milk products will create less congestion and more elimination. There are many levels of the progressive detoxification diets, from these simple changes to complete fasting.

Among the several therapies available for detoxification, some are more intrusive or less natural than others, and it is recommended that professional advice be obtained when selecting a particular programme. The most popular and effective detoxification therapies range from fasting, specific diets, vitamin therapy, colon therapy and chelation therapy to hyperthermia.

Fasting: This is certainly the least expensive and easiest therapy to attempt, but it should always be preceded by a visit to the doctor or a qualified health professional. Fasting is generally done for a limited, specific number of days. All fasting regimens permit water to be consumed, for it is essential to prevent dehydration. There are different kinds of fasting. Juice fasts are the most popular among them. The main rationale for fasting is that since far fewer toxins are ingested the body is able to rid itself of those already present.

Water and Juice Fast: Most experts recommend beginners to do one or the other over every weekend for a few months. A water-only fast starting Friday evening and ending Sunday morning (or just all day Saturday, as an alternative) should be broken with a day of raw foods (fruit/salad only, plus water), not with a heavy meal. Make sure that not less than 2–3 litres of water is consumed during the fast.

Alkaline-Detoxification Diet: Developed by Dr. Haas, this three-to-four-week plan helps to detoxify the body tissues of protein and acid wastes and can also help to reduce weight, increase vitality and promote healing. This plan involves the elimination of acid-forming foods from your diet and eating only fruits and vegetables plus fresh sprouts and millet. The diet also focuses on particular eating principles, including exceptional chewing, at least 30 to 50 times each mouthful, drinking purified water plus steamed vegetable broth and eating all food before nightfall.

Diets: Proponents say that a strong immune system founded on a plant-based diet is the best defence against environmental toxins. As opposed to fasting, detoxification, or detox diets as they are more commonly known, can be undertaken for extended periods of time. Although there are many different types of detox diets, most are based on eating organic rather than processed foods, minimising meats and maximising fruits and vegetables, and drinking filtered water. Advocates of traditional Chinese medicine also hold that certain foods, like radishes, turnips, soya beans, Swiss chard and vinegar, can actually counteract or neutralise toxins.

Vitamin Therapy: The use of antioxidants is generally recommended as an ongoing, daily aspect of people's lives, especially if they are in a compromised or particularly unhealthy environment. Some experts feel that certain vitamins, such as vitamin C and E are antioxidant in nature and are able to neutralise certain toxins called free radicals. A free radical is a particular type of atom or group of atoms that can damage cells and impair a person's immunity. While our bodies contain natural enzymes that work against these free radicals, advocates of vitamin therapy contend that vitamin C and vitamin E as well as the beta-carotene in vitamin A function as free-radical scavengers, thus neutralising the toxins that harm our immune systems.

Colon Therapy: Colonics, or cleansing the large intestine with purified water, herbs or other cleansing agents, is sometimes combined with fasting to flush out toxins from the body. A step beyond a simple enema, this procedure is performed by a trained therapist who introduces large quantities of water, or other cleansing agents, directly into the rectum using a tube and nozzle. This technique is supposed to remove toxic stool that remains in the folds of the intestine. If performed improperly or too frequently, it can be dangerous.

Chelation Therapy: The most common type of chelation therapy involves the use of a chemical agent that is recognised as being able to effectively treat heavy-metal poisoning (like lead or mercury). The synthetic drug ethylene-di-amine-tetra-acetic acid (EDTA) is administered intravenously or orally and binds to the heavy metals in the blood. The toxic metals are then flushed out naturally through the kidneys. Doctors also use natural chelating agents like zinc, garlic, vitamin C, and amino acids like cysteine. Oral chelation, while less expensive and more convenient, has been reported to work considerably slower than the intravenous method. Chelation therapy has also been used to treat artherosclerosis, or hardening of the arteries. Experts say that chelation removes calcium, which is part of the plaque that coats arteries. While some patients have reported remarkable results with this treatment, no reliable scientific data exists to support these claims. Further research is needed in the field to confirm reports of success with treating heart and cancer patients with chelation therapy.

Hyperthermia: Also known as heat stress detoxification, this technique essentially uses a sauna or a steam bath to sweat out toxic chemicals from fat cells.

Note: None of the procedures should be undertaken without medical supervision.

RECAP

- For a healthy existence the excretory, reproductive, respiratory, nervous and circulatory and digestive systems have to be maintained at their peak working conditions.
- Traditional detox regimens range from saunas, massages and body brushing to fasting, colonic irrigation and bowel enemas.
- Making simple dietary changes is the safest and perhaps most effective way to detox.

5

FASTING AS A DETOXIFYING PROCEDURE

Fasting as a method for detoxification is one of the easiest methods to cleanse the body's internal systems and organs by natural means. Fasting has a very long history, going back to biblical times. It is a traditional means of purifying the body and the mind. It can be found in cultures as diverse as the ancient Greeks and the Native Americans, and was often used as part of a rite or religious exercise. In modern times, many people fast, or do without any nutrition for a certain period of time, for health reasons or for spiritual ones. The main argument offered by those who advocate fasting is that it is a simple and inexpensive means of detoxifying the body, for getting rid of natural waste and environmental chemicals that build up in our bodies.

The other justification given for fasting is that it stimulates both the metabolism and the immune system, which helps in the process of healing and renewal. Both arguments for fasting are based on the belief that by stopping the digestive tract from having to work continuously, a major obstacle to the body's natural healing powers is removed. This, in turn, is based on the idea that it takes a great deal of energy to break down and convert the food we ingest into energy that can be spent in the process of healing the body. Proponents of fasting argue that it provides better overall health and improves vitality. The possible loss of unwanted body fat is considered a bonus.

According to naturopathy, the root cause of most of the diseases is the accumulation of toxic matter in the digestive system. Naturopaths and practitioners of alternative medicine fear an epidemic that they call bioaccumulation, or a build-up and trapping of toxic substances in the body that weakens the organs of elimination as well as the immune system and gradually affects overall health. Although both the practitioners of naturopathy and those of traditional medicine agree that the body has its own natural processes for eliminating and neutralising toxins (via perspiration, urination, exhalation and bowel movements), they disagree on the question of whether those natural systems are capable of handling the nature and amount of toxins that exist in today's world.

Those who believe that the body's systems are unable to cope with these daily poisonous assaults argue that toxins accumulate in the body faster than they can be eliminated, and are therefore the primary cause of disease. They also claim that toxic accumulation alters the body's metabolism and causes enzyme dysfunction, nutritional deficiencies, hormonal imbalances and damaged immune systems, all of which contribute to physiological and psychological decline.

Ayurveda recommends fasting as a panacea to this problem. Ayurvedic practitioners believe that it helps not only in cleansing the digestive system but also in bringing to balance all the seven constituents of the body – lymph, blood, muscle, cartilage, bone marrow, bone and sperm. During fasting, one should not undertake any strenuous mental activities and should keep the mind free from stress.

Our country has a tradition of fasting during many religious occasions. Almost every religion has a tradition of some ritualistic fasting. For instance, the Muslims fast during the month of Ramzaan, Christians during Lent and Hindus during the Navratri. Perhaps the intention behind these fasts was to inculcate a sense of discipline and abstinence in people. The benefits also extended to the resting of the digestive system. However, most of these fasts allow the consumption of food after a certain hour, which invariably leads to over-indulgence and nullifies the cleansing effects of the fast.

Apart from the ritualistic fasting, some people practise fasting at least once a week. Such fasts allow the consumption of a single meal or certain kinds of foodstuff. This gives their system a much-needed rest period but does not serve the purpose of detoxifying their digestive system.

Detoxification regimens generally start with the liver, the body's major detoxification organ. When the liver is working efficiently and effectively, other organs often follow suit.

One of the most crucial parts of the digestive system is the much-neglected organ called liver, which is also the largest organ in our body. It has an unenviable job of filtering 86 litres of blood every hour, flushing out the toxins and generating enough bile to deal with the fats we consume. Keeping the liver at peak health is paramount to the digestive process. A high level of insulin can easily damage the liver, so it is important to monitor the levels of insulin in the blood if you are a suspected diabetic. Just by drinking 10 to 12 glasses of water you can help the liver in bile production.

Once the detox process begins, digestion, brain function and other physiological processes also tend to work better. There are many types and degrees of fasting. The most popular is the juice fast in which only fresh fruit and vegetable juice is consumed. Some also drink vegetable broth and herbal teas. Since all of these liquids are high in vitamins, minerals, amino acids and natural sugars, some consider this to be a restricted diet instead of real fast. Others maintain that a true fast consists of drinking only distilled water.

Besides the ingestion of juice or water, fasts are also differentiated by their duration. A fast can last for 24 hours or for as long as one month. However, anything more than a couple of days should be considered to be a prolonged fast, and should involve the supervision and advice of a physician.

The actual detoxification process is typically broken into three stages: the elimination, the renewal and maintenance. The duration of each phase varies with the individual and his needs. The elimination process is the first step, and can begin if a person is relatively healthy and free of a serious chronic health condition such as cancer, colitis, diabetes or heart disease. The elimination phase rids the diet of potential food allergens such as citrus, coffee and other caffeine-containing beverages, dairy, eggs, sugar and sugared foods, red meat, and gluten-rich grains such as wheat, oats, barley and rye.

Some naturopathy experts recommend at least three days of eating only vegetable broth and non-starchy steamed vegetables. These alkalising foods reduce acidity and inflammation. If a person is hungry during this stage, nuts and seeds such as almonds, sunflower or pumpkin seeds, which are also alkalising, can be consumed to satisfy hunger.

Many naturopaths recommend the drinking of eight glasses of water each day in addition to fruit juices. An all-liquid diet is traditionally called a juice fast. A juice fast increases awareness and energy availability for elimination. Fresh juices literally pick up dead matter from the body and carry it away. It becomes easier to listen to your body telling you what foods and diet are right for your needs through cravings – for example, a desire for protein foods, B vitamins or minerals. This is natural biofeedback.

During this phase there is a cleaning out of mucus and toxins from the intestinal tract and major organs. Everything functions more effectively when toxins, obstructions and wastes are removed.

A three-to-seven-day cleansing programme can rid the system of excess mucus, old faecal matter, trapped cellular and non-food wastes, or inorganic mineral deposits that cause arthritis.

Fasting works by self-digestion. During a cleanse, the body decomposes and burns only the substances and tissues that are damaged, diseased or unneeded, such as abscesses, tumours, excess fat deposits and congestive wastes. Even a relatively short fast accelerates elimination, often causing dramatic changes as masses of accumulated waste are expelled. Digestion usually improves right away as do many gland and nerve functions. Cleansing also helps release hormone secretions that stimulate immune response and encourages a disease-preventing environment.

One clear sign that your body is detoxifying is when you experience short spells of headaches, fatigue, body odour, bad breath, diarrhoea or mouth sores that commonly accompany accelerated elimination.

After elimination or cleansing comes the process of rebuilding of healthy tissue and energising them. Now that the digestive tract is cleaned and spruced up, your body begins the process of rebuilding and renewal at an enhanced pace. It is important to eat only fresh and simply prepared foods during this phase so as not to burden the system or load it with any undesirable matter. The diet should be very low in fat, with no fried foods. Avoid alcohol, caffeine, tobacco and sugars. Avoid all kinds of meats, especially the red variety. Yoghurt is beneficial and light, so it can be taken in good quantity. Fruits and fruit juices play an important part, as do the fresh green vegetables.

You will notice the difference as you go through the process. The body feels light and energised. There is a feeling of wellness and energy. The final step is keeping your body clean and toxin-free. This is the maintenance stage. Don't go and binge on all restricted items the moment you get off the detoxification programme. That would be a total nullifying of the entire process after all the hard work of detoxification. Modifying lifestyle habits is the key to a strong resistant body. A diet for health maintenance relies heavily on fresh fruits and vegetables for fibre; cooked vegetables, grains and seeds for strength and alkalinity; sea foods, soy foods, eggs and low-fat cheeses as sources of protein. For complete rejuvenation, you should add a regimen of exercise and relaxation techniques.

During the maintenance phase the diet has to be strictly maintained to keep the toxin levels low. Most experts recommended the macrobiotic diet for an overall beneficial effect. The term 'macrobiotic' describes a holistic lifestyle, which seeks to empower people to take control of their lives and to educate them to make healthy lifestyle choices and decisions. Macrobiotics is based on the Chinese philosophy of yin and yang, which are two qualities that balance one another, and which exist in every natural object and cycle. Generally speaking, yin (pronounced 'yeen') foods tend to be more sugary and/or watery and/or cold or tropical in origin.

Yang (pronounced 'yahn') foods tend to be more meaty and dry, or cooked and polar in nature.

Very yang food (e.g. meat, poultry, table salt, ginseng) as well as very yin food (e.g. sugar, euphoric drugs, strong alcoholic beverages) is generally avoided in macrobiotic way of life. These foods are often called 'extreme food'. Balanced foods, which are not so 'extreme', compose the standard macrobiotic diet. Cereal grains reside at the balance between yin and yang, but even they are involved in the yin and yang classification (everything has yin and yang components; nothing is 'neutral'). Therefore, whole grains and their derivatives are considered the mainstay of the diet. All ancient civilisations had used a grain-based element as the main diet.

Macrobiotics recommends wholesome food like fresh, seasonal vegetables which are locally available. The foods to eliminate are:

- Meat, animal proteins, dairy products and eggs (including butter, yoghurt, ice cream, milk and cheese), refined sugars, chocolate, molasses, honey, other simple sugars and foods treated with them, and vanilla.
- Tropical or semi-tropical fruits and fruit juices, soda, artificial drinks and beverages, coffee, coloured tea and all aromatic stimulating teas such as mint or peppermint tea.
- All artificially-coloured, preserved, sprayed, or chemically-treated foods. All refined and polished grains, flours and their derivatives; mass-produced industrialised food including all canned, frozen and irradiated foods.

- Hot spices, any aromatic stimulating food or food accessory, artificial vinegar and strong alcoholic beverages.

Macrobiotics also recommends

- Increasing the quantity of complex carbohydrates
- Decreasing the intake of salt
- A total taboo on junk food

Macrobiotic dietary principles are based on a simple, intuitive understanding of the body's needs and the belief that proper dietary practice is essential for the development of health, freedom and happiness.

The following principles are recommended for people who live in the world's temperate zones:

- Each meal should be based on vegetable products with occasional supplements of animal food if necessary.
- Whole cereal grains should constitute more than half of the meal, with occasional supplements of beans.
- Most vegetables should be cooked rather than raw and chosen for seasonal variation. Locally-grown produce is preferable to that grown at a distance.
- Sea vegetables may be used as a supplement.
- Fruits and nuts grown in the same climate may also be used.
- Animal food should comprise less than 15 per cent of the meal and should always be eaten with vegetables.
- Food should be mainly seasoned with unrefined sea salt and vegetable oil.

Foods, which are excluded from the diet include sugar, spices and alcohol (which are said to be too much yin), and meat, eggs and cheese (which are supposed to be too much yang). These foods are generally believed to be too strong for human consumption, unbalancing the system and causing illness. The best-balanced foods containing yin and yang are:

- Yin – fruit, leafy green vegetables, nuts and seeds, tofu and tempeh, fruit and vegetable juices, jams (made without refined sugar), barley malt
- Yang – wholegrain cereals, such as brown rice, bread, flour, whole oats, root vegetables such as potatoes, parsnips and turnips, fish and shellfish, cottage cheese, beans, peas and lentils, salt, miso and shoyu soya sauce

General food suggestions:

Eat:

- Salmon, fresh tuna and shrimp for essential fatty acids, brain food and protein
- A wide variety of vegetables for minerals, vitamins, EFAs, protein and antioxidants
- Fresh vegetable salads with tomatoes, peas, cucumbers, celery and plenty of lettuces for minerals, vitamins, fibre, complex carbohydrates, antioxidants and system sweepers
- Apples, pineapples, grapes and oranges for fibre, system cleansing and hydrating

- Steamed vegetables like green beans, broccoli and cauliflower for vitamins and minerals, fibre, anti-carcinogens, complex carbohydrates and stable nerves
- Brown rice, couscous, brown rice crackers and rice cakes for B vitamins, fibre and protein
- Green tea every morning for antioxidants and detoxifiers
- Plenty of herbs and natural spices for circulation and immune response.

Avoid:

- Red meats, cured meats, organ meats, refined foods, canned foods, sugar, salt, saturated fats, coffee, alcohol and nicotine
- Over-the-counter drugs

Note: Fasting is not recommended for very weak patients, pregnant women, persons of advanced age, infants and TB patients. Several kinds of symptoms can occur during the fasting phase, such as tastelessness, bad breath, coated tongue, vomiting, mild stomach ache, giddiness and exhaustion. These symptoms occur when the body begins to throw out the toxic matter. Many novices are likely to get upset on noticing these symptoms. Some may even stop the process midway. One thing they need to know is that there is nothing wrong with the body when these kinds of symptoms occur and they should continue the fast until the tongue gets cleared, appetite becomes normal and they begin to feel energised.

RECAP

- Toxic accumulation alters the body's metabolism and causes enzyme dysfunction, nutritional deficiencies, hormonal imbalances and damaged immune systems, contributing to physiological and psychological decline.
- A clogged digestive system can throw up problems like pimples, arthritis, allergies and offensive breath, gas, stomach ache, heartburn, constipation, etc.
- Fasting, as a method for detoxification, is one of the easiest methods to cleanse the body's internal systems and organs by natural means.
- Fasting stimulates both the metabolism and the immune system; thus it promotes healing and renewal.
- A three-to-seven-day cleansing programme can rid the system of excess mucus, old faecal matter, trapped cellular and non-food wastes, or inorganic mineral deposits.
- Detoxification leads to a feeling of wellness and energy.

6

A FIBRE FIX

Fibre happens to be one of the most important elements in the detoxification process. To achieve an absolutely efficient digestive and eliminative balance, it is important to fibre up the diet.

A sluggish digestive or excretion system can cause inadequate elimination of the toxins from our body leading to various kinds of ailments, including cancer. A regular dose of fibre could keep you regular and decrease your cancer risk. Most people don't get enough fibre in their diets, which can contribute to a number of health problems – haemorrhoids, constipation and colon cancer.

In fact, a recent study found that people who suffer from frequent constipation are more likely to develop colon cancer. When a person is constipated, the colon gets more exposure to materials that could contain carcinogens. Fibre in the diet helps keep the colon clean, effectively reducing the cancer risk. Another study determined that a diet with plenty of fibre-rich whole grains could prevent other kinds of cancer, even those with nothing to do with the digestive system, such as breast, kidney or bladder cancer.

Doctors say it is not difficult to fit the 20 to 35 grams of fibre you need each day into your diet. Fruit, vegetables and many breakfast cereals provide great opportunities to expand fibre intake. However, a large increase in fibre may result in abdominal discomfort, so fibre should be added to the diet gradually over a period of three weeks. If you suffer from constipation, you may need fibre supplements. Drinking plenty of water with your fibre also helps keep your colon clean.

High-fibre benefits

Just about everyone can benefit from a low-fat, high-fibre diet. To lose weight and stay healthy, try increasing the amount of fibre in your diet. Researchers in Boston found in a recent study that young adults who eat a lot of fibre were less likely to gain weight, have lower insulin levels and generally have fewer risk factors for heart disease than those who don't eat a lot of fibre. Doctors believe part of this is because fibre slows the progress of food through the digestive system, which helps keep insulin flow low and may reduce the amount of food that is absorbed by the body. The fibre which is soluble in nature stimulates the colon's action and binds to cholesterol and harmful fats making it easier for the body to expel them. Soluble fibre is easily assimilated and can be found in fruits and vegetables as well as oat bran. Getting at least six grams of fibre per serving should be your target.

Fibre is also good for teenagers. There has been some concern about putting growing teenagers who need a lot of energy on a low-fat, high-fibre diet, but researchers have recently reported that teens that ate such a diet were more likely to get all the vitamins they needed than their peers whose diets weren't as restrictive. Doctors believe this is because the teens that ate the high-fibre diet had more variety in their food choices. Fruits, vegetables and whole grains are good sources of fibre – and also good sources of nutrition for your diet.

Fibre is much more than a detoxifier. Some of its many health benefits are:

- Diets low in saturated fat and cholesterol that include soluble fibre from whole oats may reduce the risk of heart disease.
- Diets low in saturated fat and cholesterol and rich in fruits, vegetables and grain products that contain fibre, particularly soluble fibre, may reduce the risk of coronary heart disease.
- Diets low in fat and rich in fibre-containing grain products, fruits and vegetables may reduce the risk of some types of cancer.

RECAP

- A regular dose of fibre could keep you regular and decrease your cancer risk.
- Fruits, vegetables and whole grains are good sources of fibre – and also good sources of nutrition for your diet.
- Researchers in Boston found that young adults who eat a lot of fibre were less likely to gain weight, have lower insulin levels and generally have fewer risk factors for heart disease than those who don't eat a lot of fibre.

7

JUICING IT UP

Juice therapy has been around for ages. Remember, as children when we were sick, mother plied us with glassfuls of juices of all kinds? Right from the ubiquitous sweet lemon to the orange juice and even the watermelon juice, we had it all. A visit to an ailing or recuperating person in the hospital would invariably entail carrying fruits and fruit juices. All these practices had a very strong reason behind them. Fresh fruit juices have been known to have remarkable health-promoting properties and have been used for centuries by naturopaths to help treat a range of ailments. Way back in the sixteenth century, lime juice, chock-full of vitamin C, was used as an effective cure for scurvy in the sailors who were deprived of fresh food during their long journeys at sea.

Half a century back, in the 1950s, a report by the British Ministry of Health and Public Service Laboratory stated: 'Juices are valuable in relief of hypertension, cardiovascular and kidney diseases and obesity. Good results have been obtained with large amounts, up to one litre daily, in the treatment of peptic ulceration, also in the treatment of chronic diarrhoea, colitis and toxaemia of gastro and intestinal origin . . . The high-buffering capacities of the juices reveal that they are very valuable in the treatment of hyperchlorohydria (excessive production of hydrochloric acid in the stomach). Milk has often been used for this purpose, but spinach juice, juices of cabbage, kale and parsley were found to be superior to milk for this purpose.'

These findings were eventually supported by other research results. Several laboratories around the world in their research reported significant healing of peptic ulcers when cabbage juice was administered to the patients.

Most fruits are rich in mineral content like calcium and potassium, which are a great boon in controlling premature ageing and degeneration of the body cells. Vegetable juices of bitter gourd are helpful in controlling diabetes. Wheatgrass juice is an excellent detoxifier. The juice of cucumber and onion activate the pancreas and help in the production of insulin, an essential requirement for diabetics.

Advocates of juice therapy maintain that is it a potent method of detoxifying our body. It is a simple method to flush out the toxins that invade our bodies through various agencies. By now you must have already realised how essential it is to rid the body of these toxins and what better method than one that is simple, not too costly and delicious!

Juice therapy has been found to have a rejuvenating effect on the excretory organs like liver, lungs, skin and kidneys as they begin to work more efficiently. The digestive system perks up and the assimilation of various food components is enhanced. That is not all – it supplies the body with various nutrients like vitamins, minerals and carbohydrates.

Although many experts bet on the use of water during fasting, there are an equal number of them who advocate juices, instead. Their contention is that the fruit juices, being alkaline in nature, speed up the healing effect that results from fasting. The acid–alkali level in the body also gets levelled during juice therapy. They argue that the elimination of uric acid and other inorganic acids from the body is accelerated due to juice treatment. Whether you agree with the fruit juice advocates or the water therapists is entirely your choice. But one fact that remains doubtless is that fruit juices cleanse and nourish the human system.

Another undeniable fact is that fruit juices are very easily and rapidly assimilated by the body. That would explain the glasses of juice one needs to drink while recuperating from any illness. They are also a very good source of instant energy when we are tired and depleted since the sugars like fructose, contained in fruits, are easily broken down by the body.

Although one may complain about the high cost of fruits, it is worth considering that the money spent on medicines could be exorbitant. Of course, it is better to opt for the fresh fruits than to buy the canned or bottled stuff from the supermarket. The additives in the preserved juices rob them of their nutritional value and efficacy. It is definitely worthwhile to take time off from a busy schedule to juice fresh fruits.

Fruit juices are a delicious version of tonics, offering a safe, inexpensive way to stimulate digestion, bolster the immune system and encourage the elimination of toxins.

Studies show that fruit juices can speed the healing of infections and can even help cure stomach ulcers. And when used in conjunction with other natural techniques, such as herbs, homeopathy and nutritional therapy, fresh juices can create an optimal nutritional foundation to bolster the body's innate healing abilities.

Juice advocates confirm the finding that many antioxidants and phytochemicals have a significant role in cancer prevention. Certain vegetables and fruits like cabbage, kale, broccoli, cauliflower, garlic, onions, leeks, shallots, oranges, grapefruit and lemons are especially rich in antioxidants and phytochemicals. Juice from these sources can provide you with a concentrated mixture of unique nutrients that can't be obtained from commercial supplements.

Juices made from green vegetables are said to heal, stabilise and calm frayed nerves. Wheat grass juice, made from kernels that have sprouted to resemble grass, is often recommended to detoxify the body, flush the liver and purify the blood.

Here are some fruit and vegetable juices known for their curative properties:

Apple: Apples are a rich source of sorbitol, a type of sugar used to create energy for the body and as a mild laxative. It also contains polyphenols, antioxidants thought to counteract viruses. In olden times apple juice was used for combating constipation.

Beetroot: Beetroot juice is a potent blood purifier and is very effective in curing disorders of the skin and stomach. Beets are loaded with vitamins C and E, beta-carotene, and magnesium. Beet juice is high in potassium and folic acid. It is also a natural laxative and excellent source of iron, which enables it to counteract anaemia. It contains nutrient compounds that have been found to provide protection against heart disease as well as cancer of the colon. Besides, it is a rich antioxidant.

Blueberry and Cranberry: Juices from both of these fruits are useful in treating urinary tract infections.

Cantaloupe: Cantaloupe is thought to possess anti-coagulative properties that thin the blood and are believed to aid in the prevention of heart attacks and strokes.

Carrot: The juice of carrots is a natural cleanser. It neutralises excess acid in the system and purifies the blood. Carrots are known to be rich in beta-carotene, vitamin A, B complex, E and potassium, as well as in the antioxidants glutathione and phthalide (both are considered anti-cancerous), which make it an effective cancer combatant. Carrot juice is also good for respiratory ailments and eyesight. The vitamin A content in it helps the liver in flushing out the toxins from the body.

Celery: Rich in sodium and potassium, celery contains several anti-cancerous antioxidants.

Cherry: Cherries have traditionally been used to relieve pain associated with gout.

Cucumber: Mainly used for salads, cucumber is really cooling, which is why it has given rise to the metaphor 'as cool as cucumber'. Cucumber juice stimulates the flow of urine and expels toxins from the body. It also controls high blood pressure and can be used as a face pack to remove skin blemishes and to reduce the oiliness of the skin. It is invaluable in curing digestive problems like hyperacidity and gastric ulcers.

Garlic: Garlic is renowned for its therapeutic effects. It acts as a coagulative agent, natural antibiotic and reducer of cholesterol.

Ginger: Ginger juice is thought to alleviate pain associated with migraines and motion sickness. The root of a ginger plant possesses anti-inflammatory properties. It soothes the throat and is an effective antidote to the accumulation of phlegm.

Lemon: Traditionally lemon has been used as an appetite stimulant instigating digestive juice activity and saliva flow.

Onion: It is a known blood purifier. The onion juice should be taken in conjunction with other juices like carrot juice and beetroot juice. Onion juice removes blemishes of the skin and also prevents hair loss. Apart from drinking this juice, you can apply it on the skin to clear up skin blemishes.

Orange: Oranges are rich in vitamin C, potassium and a number of other key vitamins and nutrients. It is excellent for the eyesight and provides immunity against diseases.

Papaya: Papaya is loaded with potassium and magnesium. It also contains papain, a substance that counteracts ulcers.

Parsley: Parsley is considered to be an effective treatment for bad breath. It also aids the functioning of kidney and improves eyesight.

Peach: Peaches are rich in potassium and are also thought to contain a mild laxative.

Pineapple: Pineapple juice contains the enzyme bromelain, an anti-inflammatory element. It also reduces the swelling associated with tooth extractions and sore throats.

Sage/Basil: Traditionally, most Indian homes have a tulsi plant in their courtyard. The juice of this plant has been used for centuries by our grandmother to cure various problems. The juice of the humble sage leaves is an excellent cure for respiratory problems like bronchitis, cold, cough, sinusitis, asthma as well as acidity and constipation. The black leaves are better than the green ones.

Spinach: Spinach is rich in iron, oxalic acid (which eases constipation but causes kidney stones), vitamin C, potassium and calcium. The juice of raw spinach helps in reducing the acidity caused by smoking or excessive consumption of alcohol. It has blood-building properties and is rich in laxative fibre, too. It also helps in controlling high blood pressure and anaemia besides preventing dental caries and bleeding gums.

Tomato: By now everyone is aware of the rich antioxidants present in tomato. Tomato juice reactivates a sluggish liver and has beneficial effect on most problems related to liver, digestion and skin.

Watermelon: Watermelon juice is high in potassium and effective in curing oedema. It helps to reduce water retention and high blood pressure.

RECAP

- Juice therapy is a potent detoxifying method. It is a simple method to flush out the toxins that invade our bodies through various agencies.
- Most fruits are rich in mineral content like calcium and potassium, which are a great boon in controlling premature ageing and degeneration of the body cells.
- Vegetable juices of bitter gourd are helpful in controlling diabetes.
- The juice of cucumber and onion activate the pancreas and help in the production of insulin, an essential requirement for diabetics.

▶▶

- Fruit juices are delicious version of tonics, offering a safe, inexpensive way to stimulate digestion, bolster the immune system and encourage the elimination of toxins.
- Studies show that fruit juices can speed the healing of infections and can even help cure stomach ulcers.

SECTION II

8

DETOXIFYING THE LUNGS

The importance of correct breathing has been recognised since the beginning of history. The shaman, the wise men and witch doctors of ancient times used breathing techniques to induce trances or to improve performance. In eastern medicine correct breathing is considered to be vital for good health. It is also thought to be essential if one is to progress to the higher levels of skills in meditation and martial arts and in the achievement of the asanas or postures taken up during *tai chi* and yoga exercise, for example. Today, it is generally recognised that correct breathing has an important role to play, in particular, in helping to reduce levels of stress as well as its signs and symptoms. The highly-popular Sudarshan Kriya practised by the followers of the Art of Living is also based on the tenets of pranayama.

There is growing evidence that correct breathing practised through the pranayama techniques can heal almost every ailment from eye problems, asthma and hypertension to cancer and kidney failure. Pranayama helps by ridding the body of depressive energy and tension. According to the renowned yoga expert Swami Ramdev, 'pranayama involves practising deep breaths to regulate and direct one's prana shakti. When one is going through a stressful situation, the physiology, the brain and the endocrine system are influenced negatively. Breathing techniques of pranayama establish a positive body–mind relationship. It also harnesses the energy and helps in the removal of negative thoughts leading to healthy physiology.'

The environmental strains of modern urban life have made breathing techniques even more important than they have been in the past since the air that we breathe is polluted with smoke and chemicals that are toxic in nature and can damage lung tissues. Polluted air is dangerously low in oxygen and atmospheric ions that are linked with positive health. Since it is impractical for the majority of us to start a new life in the less-polluted countryside, it is vitally important that we breathe as efficiently as possible.

When we inhale, air is drawn into the lungs, where it fills tiny air sacs that are surrounded by a network of miniscule blood vessels. The blood then absorbs the oxygen and transports it around the body to supply every cell with it. As the oxygen is absorbed, the blood passes carbon dioxide – the waste product of energy released from the cells – back into the air, to be removed from the body when we exhale.

Most of the diseases are caused due to incomplete exhalation and inhalation. Why do you think your breath becomes shallow when you are under stress? Why do you hyperventilate? These are the symptoms of high stress levels, and they cause incomplete oxygenation of our blood. The breath of life, as it is correctly called, is supposed to rejuvenate our body cells by bringing in a surfeit of oxygen to them.

Though we all breathe by instinct, most people use only about half their lung capacity, the result being that the air sacs (alveoli) absorb too little oxygen, leaving an excess of carbon dioxide in the tissues, which is reabsorbed by the blood. On the other hand, when we panic or suffer from anxiety attacks, we begin to hyperventilate. Our breathing becomes shallow and hurried and the body expels too much carbon dioxide.

Breathing is the only means to supply our bodies and their various organs with oxygen, which is vital for our survival. It is also an important method of getting rid of waste products and toxins from the body.

We all know the significance of oxygen. It is essential for the efficiency of the brain, nerves, glands and internal organs. We can do without food for weeks and without water for days, but without oxygen we will die within a few minutes. Lack of oxygen supply to the brain, even for a few minutes, can result in the destruction of all vital organs in the body.

The brain is a great oxygen-guzzler. It requires more oxygen than any other organ. If it doesn't get enough, the result is mental sluggishness, negative thoughts and depression.

Yogis realised these facts thousands of years ago, much before the modern scientists and doctors proclaimed the benefits of proper breathing. They developed and perfected various breathing techniques. These breathing exercises are particularly important for people who have sedentary jobs and spend most of the day in offices. Oxygen-starved brains lead to fatigue, nervousness and irritability. Insomnia and lowered immune system are the resultant problems. Frequent colds, flu and other infections naturally follow lowered immunity. It is a vicious cycle – the stress we face reduces efficient breathing, and the reduced intake of oxygen lowers the body's resistance to disease.

One of the major secrets of vitality and rejuvenation is purified and oxygenated blood in the body. The quickest and most effective way to purify blood is by inhaling enough oxygen. Complete oxygenation of blood leads to peak performance of every part of the body as well as the mind. The complexion becomes clearer and brighter and wrinkles begin to fade. In short, the body embarks on a programme of rejuvenation.

The Stress Effect

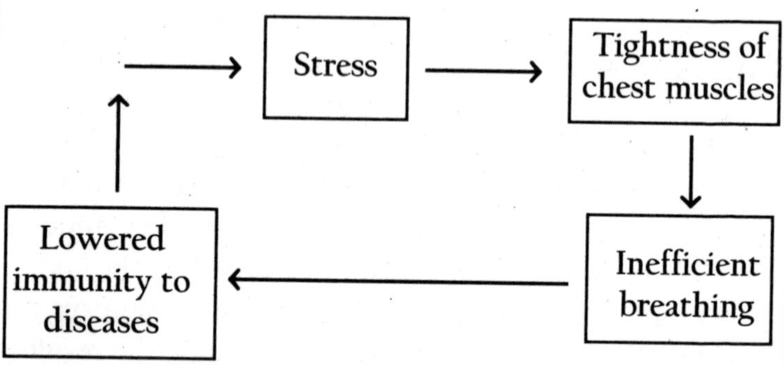

Scientists have known for a long time that there exists a strong relation between respiration and mental states. Improper breathing produces diminished mental ability. It is known that mental tensions produce restricted breathing. As our duties, responsibilities and their attendant problems become more demanding, we develop wrong breathing habits.

A normally sedentary person, when confronted with a perplexing problem, tends to lean forward, draw his arms together and bend his head down. All these body postures result in reduced lung capacity. Often, a person resorts to irregular or shallow breathing when he is extremely stressed, and the resultant body fatigue is due to the diminished level of oxygen in the blood.

Shallow breathing results in a build-up of toxins in the body. This kind of breathing does not exercise the lungs enough, so they lose some of their elasticity, causing a further reduction in vitality. We need to breathe more slowly and deeply. Quick, shallow breathing results in oxygen starvation, which leads to reduced energy, premature ageing, poor immune system and a myriad of other factors. Our resistance to disease is reduced, since oxygen is essential for healthy cells. This means we catch more colds and develop other ailments more easily.

Breathing right

Start by learning correct breathing techniques when lying down, while you are alone and without distractions. Once you have mastered the technique, it can be practised in any position, anywhere – eventually it will become a habit.

Wear loose, comfortable clothes and lie on your back on the floor using a mat, or on your bed.

Place both your hands on the lower edges of your ribs, with fingers nearly touching.

Relax your body.

Breathe in deeply and smoothly through your nostrils. Feel your diaphragm pulling out and down, your stomach rising and your ribs expanding upwards and outwards. Hold the breath for a few seconds.

Breathe out smoothly. This requires no muscular activity, since all that happens is that the diaphragm and the muscles of the chest let go, but try to ensure that all the air that you inhaled is expelled. The ribs collapse down and in; the stomach lowers.

Repeat three or four times, then relax and breathe naturally for a few minutes, before starting the sequence once again.

Note: Your shoulders should remain stationary during breathing. Many people, especially women, breathe solely into their upper lobes by raising and lowering their shoulders. This does not give the body an adequate supply of oxygen and is a common symptom of stress.

If you feel heady and faint during the breathing exercises, it is the result of the brain receiving an unusually large amount of oxygen. Relax and breathe naturally for a few minutes – the sensation will soon pass.

Benefits of deep breathing

Deep breathing produces the following benefits:

Improvement in the quality of the blood due to its increased oxygenation in the lungs: This aids in the elimination of toxins from the system. Better digestion and assimilation of food. The digestive organs, such as the stomach, receive more oxygen, and hence operate more efficiently.

Improvement in the health of the nervous system, including the brain, spinal cord, nerve centres and nerves. This is due to the increased oxygenation. The brain has a special affinity for oxygen, requiring three times more oxygen than the rest of the body. A good supply of oxygen enhances brain functioning, which in turn affects a person's sense of well-being. In addition, oxygenation of the brain tends to reduce stress.

Rejuvenation of the glands – especially the pituitary and pineal glands – takes place when there is an adequate supply of oxygen in the body. These two glands are known as the master glands since they control major body functions.

Rejuvenation of the skin is an added bonus. Efficient supply of oxygen causes smoother skin and delays facial wrinkles leading to an anti-ageing effect.

The movements of the diaphragm during the deep breathing exercise massage the abdominal organs – the stomach, small intestine, liver and pancreas. The upper movement of the diaphragm also massages the heart. This stimulates the blood circulation in these organs. The lungs become healthy and powerful, a good insurance against respiratory problems.

Deep, slow, yogic breathing reduces the workload for the heart. The result is a more efficient, stronger heart that operates better and lasts longer. It also means reduced blood pressure and fewer heart diseases.

The yogic breathing exercises reduce the workload on the heart in two ways. Firstly, deep-breathing leads to more efficient lungs, which means more oxygen is brought into contact with blood sent to the lungs by the heart. So the heart doesn't have to work as hard to deliver oxygen to the tissues. Secondly, deep breathing leads to a greater pressure differential in the lungs, which leads to an increase in the circulation, thus resting the heart a little. Deep, slow breathing assists in weight control.

If you are overweight, the extra oxygen burns up the excess fat more efficiently.

Relaxation of the mind and body is the natural outcome of slow, deep and rhythmic breathing, which causes a reflex stimulation of the parasympathetic nervous system. It also results in a reduction in the heart rate and relaxation of the muscles.

Pranayama: the breathing exercises of yoga

Pranayama, as traditionally conceived, involves much more than merely breathing for relaxation. Patanjali defines pranayama as 'the regulation of the incoming and outgoing flow of breath with retention'.

The word pranayama consists of two parts: prana and ayama. Prana is energy. It acts as physical energy, mental energy, where the mind gathers information, and as intellectual energy, where information is examined and filtered. Prana also acts as sexual energy, spiritual energy and cosmic energy. All that vibrates in this universe is prana: heat, light, gravity, magnetism, vigour, power, vitality, electricity, life and spirit are all forms of prana. Ayama means stretch, extension, expansion, length, breadth, regulation, prolongation, restraint and control, and describes the action of pranayama.

Pranayama is the breathing process or the control of the motion of inhalation, exhalation and the retention of vital energy.

During pranayama inhalation stimulates the system and fills the lungs with fresh air; retention raises the internal temperature and plays an important part in increasing the absorption of oxygen; and finally, exhalation causes the diaphragm to return to the original position and air full of toxins and impurities is forced out by the contraction of intercostal muscles. The success of pranayama depends on proper ratio being maintained between inhalation, exhalation and retention.

Anulom–vilom

This breathing technique is recommended for calming the spirit and the mind. The sun and moon are seen here as symbols of the positive and negative, and this technique shows you how to inhale the positive energy of the sun and exhale the negative waste products of the body.

Sit in an upright position – cross-legged if you can manage it. Otherwise sit on a firm-backed chair.

Pinch your nostrils shut with your right hand, the thumb closing the right nostril and the index and middle finger closing the left nostril. Only gentle pressure is needed, so do not pinch too hard.

Breathe through your mouth as you practise opening and closing the nostrils alternately.

When you have learnt how to do this, inhale deeply and slowly as for the basic method through your right nostril – keep the left nostril firmly closed.

Hold for the count of time it took you to inhale – if you feel uncomfortable, let it go.

Exhale gradually through your left nostril again for the same length of time it took to inhale. The comparative ratio for these three motions – breathing in, holding, then breathing out – is therefore 1:1:1. This rhythm can take a while to master, but the control it engenders and the results are worthwhile. Traditionally, practitioners of advanced yoga use a ratio of 1:4:2, but without specialised training you should not try to go beyond 1:2:2.

Repeat five times. Next use the left nostril to inhale and the right nostril to exhale and repeat for five times.

Breathe twice through both nostrils deeply and fully.

Relax totally in the same position and feel the tension disappearing.

The benefits

This exercise gives complete control of the respiratory process. The lungs operate efficiently. Respiratory problems like asthma and allergies disappear.

With practice, one is able to master the flow of energy into the body.

There is complete clarity of the mind.

The endocrine system begins to function optimally as the flow of hormones is regularised.

Anulom–vilom is known to cure headache and migraine.

It is said that proper and regular practice or anulom–vilom

can stabilise blood pressure and check depression.

It can control stress, reduce fatigue, galvanise brain functioning and bring about a happy mental state.

Nadi shuddhi pranayama

Sit erect and comfortably in any meditative posture.

Be calm and close your eyes.

Close the right nostril with the right thumb.

Now inhale slowly through the left nostril and fill your lungs.

After complete inhalation, press the left nostril with the ring finger of the right hand and close the left nostril.

Open the right nostril and exhale slowly. After complete exhalation, again inhale through the right nostril and fill your lungs.

Close the right nostril by pressing it with the right thumb.

After opening the left nostril, breathe out slowly. This completes one round of Nadi Shudhi pranayama.

The benefits

Cleanses and tones up entire nervous system.

Those who suffer from cold and cough frequently especially benefit from this pranayama.

It strengthens the heart.

It clears up blocked nostrils.

Removes mental tension and worries

Cures headaches

Induces a feeling of peace

Kapalbhati

Sit comfortably in any meditative posture.

Exhale through both nostrils, contracting the middle and lower abdomen portions.

Release the contractions quickly and immediately. Follow with another forceful exhalation.

Inhale passively and effortlessly.

Gradually increase the frequency to about 100 strokes per minute.

After the round take a deep breath and exhale gradually.

The benefits

It cleanses the capillaries of the remotest part of the body.

It purifies the frontal section of the brain.

It helps in cleaning the nasal passages.

It aids in combating asthma, diabetes, chronic bronchitis and nervous disorders.

In fact, the exponents claim that Kapalbhati is one of the most effective breathing techniques that can control and heal almost every ailment and help in weight reduction too.

It brings alertness and sharp thinking and improves memory.

It is especially beneficial for controlling all respiratory-tract-related problems.

Sukha pranayama

Sit comfortably in any meditative posture.

Keep the palms on the knees and observe your natural breathing.

Feel the breath flowing and out of the lungs. Let the breathing be natural.

Feel the abdominal movement while breathing.

While inhaling, let the abdominal wall move out and while exhaling let it move in.

Keep your mind clear, only observing your breathing.

While inhaling, visualise the flowing in of power and energy and while exhaling visualise your body throwing out all stress and diseases.

The benefits

It provides deep relaxation to the body and mind.

Strengthens the nervous system and respiratory system.

Improves concentration.

Relieves stress, depression and hypertension.

Sheetali

Sit comfortably in any meditative posture.

Keep both palms on the knees in *Jnana Mudra*.

Stick out the tongue. Roll it up from the sides to form a tubular shape.

Slowly suck the air through it and fill the lungs completely.

After full inhalation withdraw the tongue and close the mouth.

Hold the breath for some time and then slowly exhale through the nose.

Repeat at least five times.

The benefits

Useful in treating fever.

Good for liver, spleen, and is a good blood purifier.

Reduces tension and high blood pressure.

Cools the nervous system.

RECAP

- Most of the diseases are caused due to incomplete exhalation and inhalation.
- Correct breathing can heal almost every ailment from eye problems, asthma, and hypertension to cancer and kidney failure.
- Pranayama is the breathing process or the control of the motion of inhalation, exhalation and the retention of vital energy.

9

THE CORRECT MODE OF BREATHING

While sitting

This is especially important for people who have deskbound jobs and spend many hours in a seated position.

Make sure you are sitting comfortably with your spine straight.

Relax your shoulders and place your hands loosely on your lap.

Breathe using the same basic method as for lying down.

Feel the air filling your lungs, right down to the bottom lobes.

Check your shoulders – they should not be moving up and down.

If you feel that you are not filling your lungs fully, place your hands on the bottom edge of the ribs, and over the stomach and check that your ribs and stomach are expanding fully under your fingers as you breathe in.

Breathe in this manner a few times until you sense the movement and then return your hands to your lap.

While walking

Many of us tend to hold back our breath while walking. Here are some tips to help you make the best use of atmospheric oxygen while walking.

Walk at a steady pace, letting your hands swing loosely by your side.

Breathe in deeply – as in the basic method – for a certain number of paces, hold the breath for half that number and breathe out gradually for the same number. Find which number of paces feels right for you.

Maintain the rhythm and repeat the exercise five times. Then relax and breathe naturally.

Repeat the whole exercise a few times during each walk.

The healing breath

The Healing breath is a popular method of healing used in all branches of eastern medicine. It involves breathing in the *chi*, as Chinese and Japanese medicine calls the 'life force', or the prana, as Indian medicine names it, into the lungs and visualising it flowing from them first into the solar plexus and then to the area to be healed. During exhalation the disease is visualised flowing out of the body.

The re-energising breath

These two exercises in breathing will first perform a releasing function on your body and mind and then recharge them. The second exercise is especially structured to boost your vitality, but it should be used sparingly to prevent hyperventilation.

Breathe in deeply through an open mouth and sigh out with a relaxed throat.

Your upper back widens on inhale and releases on exhale.

Don't worry if you yawn; it's your body's homeostatic mechanism correcting your oxygen and carbon dioxide balance.

Open your mouth wide, inhale deeply and let the air out in a big 'hah'.

Repeat a few times quickly. If you feel light-headed, breathe normally through your nose.

Tingling in your mouth or fingers is a normal reaction to shifting levels of oxygen and carbon dioxide.

Tension-releasing breath

This exercise is particularly useful, since it only takes a few minutes and can be performed anywhere, at any time.

Stand up with your hands hanging loosely by your side.

Breathe in slowly through your nostrils, tensing all your muscles at the same time.

Hunch your shoulders up to your ears, clench your hands as hard as possible, tighten your stomach muscles, clench your buttocks and raise yourself up on to tiptoe.

Hold this position to the count of five. Fix your eye on something straight ahead to help you balance.

Slowly breathe out through your nostrils and at the same time relax all your muscles, so that by the time you have fully exhaled your shoulders are down, your hands are floppy, your stomach is relaxed and your knees are slightly bent.

Repeat five times.

De-stressing breath

The more stressed out we are, the tighter we hold ourselves, especially in the jaw, chest and diaphragm. If we breathe deeply, the oxygen flows freely, and we can think and feel more clearly.

This exercise will help you de-stress and unwind.

Sit cross-legged on the floor, or in a chair with your feet flat on the ground, head straight and chin parallel to the floor.

Inhale slowly through your nose, filling your abdomen, ribs and chest. Then blow out steadily though puckered lips until your lungs are empty.

Breathe in again, feeling your torso muscles move like bellows. Imagine expelling tension from your body.

RECAP

- Breathing is the only means to supply our bodies and their various organs with oxygen. It is also an important means of getting rid of waste products and toxins from the body.
- Our vitality and rejuvenation depends on the amount of oxygen in the blood stream.
- There is a strong connection between respiration and mental states. Improper breathing produces diminished mental ability.
- Shallow breathing results in a build-up of toxins in the body.
- Quick shallow breathing results in oxygen starvation, which leads to reduced vitality, premature ageing, and poor immune system. We catch more colds and develop other ailments more easily.

▸▸

- ➥ Correct breathing helps to reduce levels of stress and control many ailments.
- ➥ Pranayama techniques can heal almost every ailment from eye problems, asthma and hypertension to cancer and kidney failure.

10

HELPING THE SKIN TO DETOXIFY

The skin is the largest organ of the body and one of the first lines of defence against external pathogens, such as chemicals and poisons. It is one of the key pathways in eliminating toxins from the body. It also performs several important roles in protecting your health.

Most of us are probably aware of its role in temperature control. When we get too warm, we start to perspire, which provides a rapid means of evaporative cooling. What many of us probably don't realise is that an important detoxification process also happens when we perspire as toxins are released through the skin along with the sweat.

Many traditional tribal cultures have recognised the importance of the skin in protection of health. Indigenous practices have included sweat-baths or heated lodges as part of regular tribal healing. Romans had constructed massive saunas and baths to rejuvenate themselves. The Russians, the Turks and the Scandinavians have used this treatment for centuries.

Our skin is permeable, and can absorb toxins directly from the environment. Caustic chemicals, such as alkaline solutions, can also penetrate the skin. Once a chemical has penetrated the stratum corneum (the most superficial layer of skin), it moves through the epidermis and into the dermis. Then the rich blood supply of the dermis readily transports the chemical into the bloodstream. But the skin is not only an avenue for the absorption or release of toxins, but a detoxifying agent in its own right. Like the liver and lungs, the skin also has the ability to transform toxins from lipid-soluble, or oil-based compounds, into water-soluble forms, which can then be removed by the kidneys.

The skin has the ability to excrete toxins. Regular use of sauna and steam baths encourages the discharge of toxins through sweat.

Did you know that every day an estimated 450 grams of toxins leave the body in sweat, carried out through the skin? This is possible, however, only if the pores through which sweat travels are open. Every day our skin cells regenerate as old ones die and new ones are created. As we age, the process slows down, and as skin cells die, new ones which replace them don't appear as rapidly. Specifically, this means the dead cells are now pushed off the surface, so it's harder for them to shed, and they build up. Cosmetically speaking, this creates a dull appearance; in terms of detox, blockages are caused that reduce the amount of toxins excreted from the cells.

11

SAUNA

Sauna has been a tradition in Finland for more than a thousand years. These days almost every hotel boasts of a sauna in its premises. A sauna is nothing but a special kind of bath for thorough cleansing of the body coupled with relaxation. It works on the principle that dry heat causes sweating and copious perspiration eliminates the toxins from the body. In the ancient times stones were heated on top of a furnace to create the dry heat and the temperature in the room ranged from 80–100^{0} C. People would either sit or lie on wooden benches, exchanging gossip and enjoying themselves while their bodies perspired profusely. After this, they would take a cold shower or swim in cold water to bring down the body temperature. This was followed by a resting period to allow the body temperature to return to normal.

In the modern version of sauna, other heat-generating methods may have replaced stones, but the principle behind sauna treatment remains the same. Sauna rids the body of dirt and grime more thoroughly than ordinary bath. Many cultures use sauna cleansing as a regular part of detoxification and cleansing. It is a powerful method of eliminating environmental chemicals that are stored in fat cells. Sauna is the best method for detoxifying heavy metals; though, if you're suffering from exposure to heavy metals, you must work with a health practitioner trained in this system of detoxification.

The use of saunas (dry heat) or steam baths (wet heat) creates sweat intentionally for therapeutic purposes. This 'sweat [hyperthermic] therapy' not only releases toxins from the skin, but also relaxes muscles by easing aches and pains. Releasing toxins via the skin through perspiration removes the load from the kidneys and liver, so those with impaired liver or kidney function may safely detoxify in this manner. However, if a person does not have access to a sauna or steam bath, a person may want to create his or her own detoxification bath at home. This is prepared by filling a clean tub with hot filtered water (a shower filter or whole house filter is recommended) as hot as one can tolerate. Then add one of the following therapeutic substances to the bath:

1. Epsom salts: Start with 1/4 cup and gradually increase to as much as 900 to 1800 grams in a tub full of water.
2. Ginger root: Place half inch slices in boiling water; turn off the heat, and steep for 30 minutes. Remove the ginger, and pour the water into the tub.

For those who use a bucket instead of a tub, reduce the amount proportionately.

Some tips on sauna

The right kind of dry heat sauna is one that has not been treated with toxic chemicals.

Sauna therapy should not be taken on a hungry stomach nor should your stomach be full. Wait for at least two hours after your meal.

Exercise for 20 to 30 minutes. Cardiovascular exercise, such as running or using a treadmill or exercise bicycle, is necessary to stimulate the circulation of blood and lymph to the deep tissues.

The recommended length of time in the sauna varies according to the condition. Sittings of about 15 minutes at a time are recommended in a low-temperature sauna.

In advanced sauna cleanses, up to 45 minutes at a time is recommended, but it is essential that the sauna be low temperature and the person stays hydrated with water and minerals. Heavy sweating after 10 to 15 minutes is a sign that the sauna is too warm.

Consult a doctor before you take a sauna therapy.

Before a sauna session

Avoid heavy meals two hours before a sauna session. Avoid alcohol or other intoxicating substances. Drink eight ounces of water before entering a sauna. Add sea salt and two tablespoons of kelp daily to the diet, especially if your drinking water is mineral-free. Remove all metal jewellery before entering the sauna, as they may become very hot.

During a sauna session

Wear light clothing in a hot-air sauna. Use a small towel to wipe off the sweat. Sit on another towel. Place a third towel on the floor to avoid slipping. It is better to avoid talking or working while in a sauna. Instead use your time to meditate or relax.

To enhance the effects of a sauna session, visualise your body absorbing the heat and energy. Deep, slow breathing and good posture are very helpful. Sound therapy such as listening to soft music is also relaxing. Aromatherapy is a very effective way to enhance the relaxation effect during a sauna session.

If the sauna you are using has infrared heat bulbs to create dry heat, turn your body regularly every few minutes, so that the entire body is heated evenly. Sit on a stool or a chair without a back. Avoid touching the hot bulbs. Do not let water, towel or clothing touch the hot bulbs. The body does not get tanned in an infrared sauna, though the skin may seem to redden immediately after the therapy.

Duration

How long one remains inside a sauna depends on one's condition. Body temperature should not increase more than four degrees. The pulse should not increase by more than 50 per cent of the resting pulse. Begin with 15 minutes if you are unwell. If the heart begins to race, sweating stops or you feel very faint, end the session immediately. 60 minutes is the maximum time one should remain in the sauna, though it is not recommended that you spend such a long time inside sauna.

Ending

After you have finished your sauna, take a shower, warm or cool but not hot. Avoid soap if possible as soap leaves a film and clogs the pores of the skin. Wipe off the sweat with a skin brush or loofah. Brush all over the body including the face and hair. At first it may be a little uncomfortable, but soon it begins to feel wonderful. Brushing enhances the cleansing effect. Use shampoo and conditioner only if needed. Most of them contain chemicals that are toxic in nature. Also skip most oils, lotions and creams. These also contain chemicals that may clog the pores.

Remember to drink at least eight ounces of water after a sauna session. Relax for at least 10 minutes after the treatment, before you begin your schedule. These simple steps allow the body to reap the full benefit of the sauna experience.

Healing reactions

Healing reactions are temporary symptoms that occur as toxic substances are eliminated and chronic infections heal. Symptoms vary from mild odours, tastes or rashes to periods of fatigue, bowel changes, aches, pains or headaches. Most healing symptoms are benign. Consult a medical practitioner if any of the symptoms persists.

Emotional healing also takes place during sauna therapy. Temporary anxiety or other emotional states may occur and usually pass quickly. Some are directly related to elimination of toxic substances. Others are associated with emotional clearing.

Supervision and safety

Saunas are safe for most people, provided one follows the rules given above. Always move slowly and carefully in and around a sauna. Accidents often occur due to slippery surfaces.

Supervision is required if one has a health condition. If debilitated or very heat-sensitive, begin with less time in a sauna. The presence of an attendant or friend is also helpful.

Consult a doctor if one has any serious health condition. Those who have used LSD or other psychotropic drugs require an attendant close by, as removal of drugs from tissue storage sites may cause flashbacks and even full-blown LSD trips.

Pregnant women and children under five should avoid saunas. Young children must be accompanied by an adult. Continue prescribed medication while taking saunas unless directed otherwise by the prescribing physician.

For acute infections

If one has an acute infection with fever or other acute symptoms, more frequent, shorter sauna sessions are better until the infection subsides. Always check with someone knowledgeable if you are unsure about sauna use, although saunas are quite safe.

Besides the fact that sauna helps the skin to detoxify, it is a de-stressing and soothing experience. The other factor that goes in favour of this treatment is that it has no side effects. This simple treatment helps the skin eliminate toxins, dead cells and stimulates circulation. It helps stimulate the lymphatic system as well to eliminate toxins through the skin.

Note: Persons with high blood pressure and pregnant women should check with their doctors before using sauna therapy. It's also important to take a good supplemental mineral tablet if you're taking more than an occasional sauna, as well as drinking plenty of filtered water.

RECAP

- Our skin is permeable, and can absorb toxins directly from the environment.
- Like the liver and lungs, the skin also has the ability to transform toxins from lipid-soluble, or oil-based compounds, into water-soluble forms, which can then be removed by the kidneys.
- The skin performs the task of detoxification through perspiration.

▶▶

- An estimated 450 grams of toxins leave the body in sweat, carried out through the skin, every day.
- Regular use of sauna and steam baths encourages the discharge of toxins through sweat.
- Sauna is the best method for detoxifying heavy metals.

12

THE LYMPHATIC SYSTEM

The lymphatic system is an integral part of the cleansing process in the body. It is the garbage collector, the internal vacuum cleaner sucking up metabolic garbage, toxins and excess fluid from the extracellular fluid of every organ. If this flow is impaired, the fluid becomes thick and toxic.

The lymphatic system is connected to every organ of the body, but its function is completely different from that of the cardiovascular system. Some of the organs that are part of the lymphatic system are lymph nodes and lymph veins, the tonsils, adenoids, appendix and the spleen. The lymph glands swell up whenever there is an infection in the body. Swollen glands, with which most of us are familiar, are symptomatic of blocked lymph nodes, which indicate a breakdown in the mechanical functioning of the lymphatic system.

When the lymphatic system gets clogged, the parts of the body that rely on it for elimination become less efficient and sluggish as they fill with their own waste. This otherwise life-sustaining system now becomes a breeding ground for infection. When the fluid enters the bloodstream, as is part of the normal process, infection can now spread to any organ or part of the body. Many viruses, bacteria and parasites stay locked within the lymphatic system when these conditions are present. The result: physical ailments, degenerative disease, hastening of the ageing process, even death!

Move your lymph to help detoxify your body

The lymphatic system is not connected up to the heart, so it has to rely upon some other activity to create the necessary pumping action it needs to circulate.

The lymphatic system is filled with millions of one-way valves, which allow lymph fluid to flow unidirectionally – usually upward against gravity. Almost anything that can stimulate the movement of lymph fluid inside the lymph vessels of the system is healthy. The three most important methods of lymphatic circulation are external massage, muscle activity and vigorous exercise.

A congested lymphatic system can lead to several health problems like eczema and other skin conditions, allergies, chronic sinusitis, heart diseases, fibrocystic disease, chronic fatigue, repetitive infections, multiple sclerosis, oedema, inflammations, high blood pressure, viral infections, puffy eyes, low back pain, cancer, ear or balance problems, arthritis, headaches, cellulite and excessive sweating.

Some of the simple methods to speed up lymph flow like body brushing, contrast showers and massage are given in the following pages.

13

BODY BRUSHING

Body brushing is the latest fad across the globe. It is almost like a cult in some societies. It isn't such a new phenomenon either. Women in our country have been using loofahs for centuries while bathing. The loofahs were used for scrubbing away dead cells of the skin to bring about a natural glow and a healthy look. It is just that the grandma's bathing technique has suddenly been rediscovered by the modern women.

Body brushing has a lot going for itself. The brushing therapy can actually work in many ways, and although most of us manage to notice the healthy and natural glow that comes after the process, not many know that there is a scientific basis to it. It can effectively combat the build up of lactic acid. It also helps in the elimination of toxins accumulated in the body. Sore muscles or stiff joints are generally the outcome of a lactic acid build up. Body brushing helps in controlling the build up.

Most of our problems arise due to stressed and tight muscles, which bunch up unhealthily to create all kinds of aches and pains in various areas of the body. Body brushing is quite an effective method of controlling the stress in the muscles and loosening them up. Another benefit from body brushing is the control of lymph build-up. The lymph nodes, which sometimes have an overflow of the lymph, can be relieved of the build-up through body brushing.

Some of the major advantages of body brushing are:

It can improve the functioning of the glands, which results in imparting a glow to the body.

It helps the skin in detoxification.

The boost in circulation helps in making the skin look taut and healthy. It also removes the debris that clogs the pores.

The exfoliation of dead skin works wonders for the skin. Since brushing helps in cell sloughing, the skin looks young and supple. Body brushing also helps the muscles recover from fatigue.

The texture and quality of the skin improve by regular brushing. The massaging action brings about a feel-good factor by soothing the muscles.

The cellulite problem can also be resolved by regular body brushing.

Does anyone need more reasons for body brushing? But, those of you who suffer from skin ailments, high blood pressure or heart problems, need to check it out with your doctor before you proceed.

While there are generally no hard and fast rules for body brushing, a few ground rules could be followed in order to make the process more effective.

You can use any kind of brush that stimulates the blood circulation and helps in getting rid of the dead skin cells. Brushes can be made of animal hair, plastic, or you may simply use a piece of jute or hemp.

Loofahs, which have been pretty popular in our country, work very well and are economical.

Use a rough piece of cloth sprinkled with salt for scrubbing. There are many who swear by the seaweeds or essential essences. If you must use them, check out the one that works best for you. Hold the brush or the cloth firmly with one hand and start brushing in vertical to horizontal and circular motions.

The movements should be directed towards the heart. Start from the bottom and work upwards. Begin from the soles and work towards the top, till you reach the chest and shoulders. Avoid the face, breasts, and other sensitive areas. Skin brushing can be done in the morning or evening, by itself or before a contrast shower. Don't get carried away while brushing. The movements should be gentle, but firm. Avoid very hard rubs. Rough handling could work adversely by irritating the skin or bruising it. At the end of the brushing, you should be able to feel a gentle tingling sensation.

14

CONTRAST SHOWERS

One of the recent developments in the field of detoxification is the contrast shower, wherein the contrasting temperatures of hot and cold water increases microcirculation through body tissues. These showers are believed to promote detoxification and strengthen the immune system. The shower helps bring nutrients, oxygen and immune cells to damaged and stressed tissues and carries away metabolic waste, inflammatory by-products and other toxic substances. Contrast showers also pep up the metabolism by stimulating the muscles and nerves in the body.

Apart from the beneficial effects on the skin, a hot-and-cold shower also speeds up the flow of lymph in the body. Lymph is a major detoxification fluid, which bathes the body cells and carries away all potentially harmful bacteria and viruses from the body. The lymphatic system is a major protection against diseases. For the system to be efficient it is necessary that the lymph is kept moving through the body. This is where the contrast showers help.

Start with three minutes of hot water followed by less than one minute of cold water. Repeat this pattern at least once, always finishing with cold (e.g. 3 minutes hot–1 minute cold–3 minutes hot–1 minute cold).

Using aerobic exercises for detoxification

Aerobic exercise simultaneously increases the discharge of toxins through sweat and increases the metabolic rate at which toxins are processed by increasing the amount of oxygen, making the most of the skin's role in protecting health.

RECAP

- The lymphatic system is an integral part of the cleansing process in the body. It functions like a garbage collector.
- When the lymphatic system gets clogged, the parts of the body that rely on it for elimination become less efficient and sluggish as they fill with their own waste.
- To keep the lymphatic system working at the peak level, it is necessary to make the lymph move more efficiently.
- Therapies like body brushing, contrast showers and massage help in keeping the lymph moving.
- Body brushing can effectively combat the build-up of lactic acid.
- It also helps in the elimination of toxins accumulated in the body.
- Sore muscles or stiff joints are generally the outcome of a lactic acid build-up. Body brushing helps in controlling the build-up.

- ➥ Body brushing is an effective method of controlling the stress in the muscles and loosening them up.
- ➥ Contrast shower increases microcirculation through body tissues. They are believed to promote detoxification and strengthen the immune system.

15

MASSAGE AND DETOXIFICATION

Massage is a holistic therapy. It affects both the body and the mind. Massage increases the circulation of blood and flow of lymph. The direct mechanical effect of rhythmically applied manual pressure and movement used in massage can dramatically increase the rate of blood flow. Also, the stimulation of nerve receptors causes the blood vessels (by reflex action) to dilate, which also facilitates blood flow. This has profound influence on one's health.

Massage is also known to cause changes in the blood. The oxygen capacity of the blood can increase by 10–15 per cent after massage. Massage affects muscles throughout the body. It can help loosen contracted, shortened muscles and can stimulate weak, flaccid muscles.

Massage also provides a gentle stretching action to both the muscles and connective tissues that surround and support the muscles and many other parts of the body, which helps keep these tissues elastic. There are noticeable effects on the nervous system. Massage balances the nervous system by soothing or stimulating it, depending on which effect is needed by the individual at the time of the massage.

These are the commonly known benefits of massage. Very few people realise that massage is also a very potent method for detoxification. It increases the body's secretions and excretions. There is a proven increase in the production of gastric juices, saliva and urine. There is also increased excretion of nitrogen, inorganic phosphorus and sodium chloride (salt). This suggests that the metabolic rate increases after a massage session. It enhances the skin health. Massage directly improves the function of the sebaceous (oil) and sweat glands, which keep the skin lubricated, clean, cooled, besides stimulating the excretion of toxins.

When the muscles are overworked, as in exercising sessions, waste products like lactic acid are accumulated in the muscles which cause stiffness, soreness and even spasms. Massage, by virtue of pepping up the circulation, increases the blood flow bringing fresh oxygen to the body tissues. This helps in the elimination of waste products, speed healing after injury, and enhances recovery from disease. By speeding up the disposal of waste products and enhanced cell nutrition, massage also helps in normalisation and greater elasticity of tissues and better flexibility of the muscles.

By virtue of accelerating the oxygen supply to the body and increasing the flow of lymph in it, massage therapy speeds up the process of detoxification. There are different methods of massage adopted by various countries around the world, including the Ayurveda technique. Even the most basic massage, like the weekly oil massage that most Indians had followed in the past, is very effective in toning the body and throwing out the toxic elements.

RECAP

- Massage is a very potent method for detoxification. It increases the body's secretions and excretions.
- There is increased excretion of nitrogen, inorganic phosphorus, and sodium chloride (salt) after a massage session.
- Massage directly improves the function of the sebaceous (oil) and sweat glands, which keep the skin lubricated, clean, cooled, besides stimulating the excretion of toxins.

16

AYURVEDIC DETOXIFICATION

According to Ayurveda, each of us has a unique constitution, determined by the balance of three vital energies in the body, known as the three *doshas* or *tridosha*. The three *doshas* are known by their Sanskrit names as *vatha*, *pitha* and *kapha*. *Pitha* is fire; it relates to the metabolism, digestion, enzymes, acid and bile. *Vatha* is the driving force; it relates mainly to the nervous system and the body's energy. *Kapha* is linked to water in the mucous membranes, phlegm, moisture, fat and lymph.

Everyone's constitution is governed by these *doshas* in varying degrees, but each of us is also controlled by one or possibly two *doshas*. Your *dosha* determines not only your constitution and the illnesses to which you might succumb, but your temperament, the colour of your hair, your tendency to put on weight and which type of foods you should eat. In short, each aspect of our everyday life is affected by the *dosha*.

You keep healthy when all three *doshas* work in balance. *Prakruthi* is the state in which we were born with levels of the three *doshas* that were just right for us. But, as we go through life, diet, environment, stress, trauma and injury cause the *doshas* to become imbalanced, a state known as the *vikruthi* state. When this imbalance becomes excessively high or low, it can lead to ill health. Ayurvedic practitioners strive to restore each individual to their *prakruthi* state.

In Ayurveda good digestion is considered the key to good health; poor digestion produces *ama*, a toxic substance believed to cause illness. *Ama* is seen in the body as a white coating on the tongue, but it can also line the colon and clog blood vessels. *Ama* is caused when the metabolism is impaired due to an imbalance of *agni*. *Agni* is the fire element which, when working normally, maintains all functions. Imbalanced *agni* is caused by irregularities in the *doshas* and such things as eating and drinking too much of the wrong foods and repressing emotions. *Agni* also ensures that the 'three *malas*' are working effectively. The *malas* are the products of the body's elimination system: sweat, urine and faeces. Body waste serves several purposes, all of which are vital to healthy functioning. For example, smooth and steady passage of faeces is also essential to maintain muscle tone in the intestines. Sweating cleanses and helps to normalise body temperature. Urine removes toxins from the body.

Ayurveds believe that it is essential to detoxify the body before prescribing restorative treatment. One of the most effective methods of detoxification is the *purwakarma*, which is increasingly gaining popularity in all health clubs and clinics. The first step is *snehana* that involves massaging herbal oils into the skin to help eliminate toxins. It can be used to treat disorders such as stress, anxiety, insomnia, arthritis or circulation problems. Next comes *swedana*, meaning sweating. Steam baths encourage the elimination of toxins through the pores and together with the oil treatments make the detoxification more effective.

Panchakarma: Panchakarma is a unique experience that leaves the mind and body feeling relaxed and rejuvenated. Our bodies are governed by their own unique rhythms and the rhythms of the environment such as weather patterns and seasonal changes. They also respond to what we put into them, and the situations and circumstances in which we live and work.

Toxicity can come from our food, our relationships and our environment, even from our own thought patterns. Over time, possibly many years, unless we consciously work to lessen those experiences, there is a build-up of toxicity at all levels, physical, mental, emotional and spiritual. Many illnesses result from the build-up of toxins in the body that can impair the functioning of its natural defences such as the lymph, circulatory and immune systems.

Panchakarma is the process by which we can purify and lessen the degenerating influences of those experiences and toxic materials. It has to be said though that receiving or undergoing those therapies or treatments will be more successful and effective if consideration and thought is given to one's lifestyle in general. However, unlike other detoxification programmes, *panchakarma* is a gentle process that achieves deep cleansing without discomfort, allowing the rejuvenating energies of the body to flow freely.

It is recommended on a seasonal basis to maintain and promote well-being in healthy people, and when needed, to restore balance in those suffering from illness.

Our bodies have natural ways for removing toxins, and *panchakarma* treatments enhance its ability to do so. Some of the toxins accumulated in the body are water-soluble, and so when we drink lots of water, it will keep cells hydrated and provide the medium (water) for easy removal of water-soluble toxins via kidneys (urine) and skin (perspiration). However, some toxins need an oil-based medium to break them down so that they can move to the gastrointestinal tract and the skin to be eliminated.

Panchakarma works to provide this by using oils to suit a specific body type. By removing those toxins it allows the body to come into balance, thus encouraging the body's own rejuvenating and healing ability to do the rest.

In order that the five actions are performed correctly, it is vital that a qualified Ayurvedic doctor gives the treatment. An inexperienced professional can do more harm than good.

People with various chronic or acute medical problems are prescribed a series of regular, specific *panchakarma* treatments in order to control their problems and rejuvenate the whole body.

Panchakarma consists of three stages known as:

Poorva-karma – Preparation Phase

Paschat-karma – Treatment Phase

Pradana-karma – Maintenance Phase

1. Poorva-karma

This preparatory phase helps to clear the channels (*srotas*) of the toxic overload, and move the imbalanced bio-energy to its sites for elimination.

Poorva-karma is designed to prepare the body for elimination of imbalances. It is performed in two parts: *snehana* or oleation and *swedana*, heat treatment, which is also used as an Ayurvedic massage treatment. According to Ayurveda, pure herbalised oils are able to permeate the cells and tissues and encourage the release of stored toxins.

There are many different herbal oil blends used for *poorva-karma*. It is an art and science in itself to be able to prepare and apply them for individual needs.

Snehana: In *snehana*, a generous application of different kinds of herbal oils is used to cover the entire body, after which massage is performed.

Swedana: This is herbal steam therapy. The heat of the steam helps to relieve tension and allows toxins that have been loosened beneath the skin to be 'sweated out'. Cloth poultices packed with herbs, powders and oils cooked in milk are freshly packed and are steaming hot when massaged into the body.

This is a treatment that generally follows the full body massage. Excluding the head and neck areas, which contain delicate organs and centres, steam-containing vapours of detoxifying and balancing herbs is given to the whole body. This helps the toxic impurities to easily leave the body. Thus, their elimination from the body becomes easier. It also moisturizes and rehydrates the skin making it soft and smooth, adding to the benefits of massage.

2. Paschat-karma

This is the main Ayurvedic treatment method. It consists of:

***Vireka* (Herbal Laxative therapy)**: The regular intake of oral laxatives at certain intervals helps to revitalise digestion and metabolic processes. It helps to reestablish the proper *agni* – metabolic power – which is the primary factor in Ayurveda. Proper digestion and metabolism at every level of our body prevents toxic overload and revitalises body tissues and enhances our resistance to disease.

***Vamana* (Emesis Therapy)**: It is the therapy where carefully controlled vomiting is induced. It helps to clear chronic congestion from various parts of the body, particularly from the chest and abdomen. The stomach is a major site for *kapha* in the physiology. Cleansing of this area is required as it reduces *ama* (toxins).

***Nasya* (Inhalations with Ayurvedic medical preparations)**: This process is used to cleanse all blocked sinuses and clear airways for proper breathing. When airways are blocked, breathing is difficult, and this necessitates an extra amount of energy. To begin with, a vigorous head/neck massage is given and then herbalised oil is gently introduced in each nostril. The *nasya* therapy also helps to clear the mental pathways and improve clarity of the mind and emotion. Conditions such as anxiety, insomnia and headaches can also be relieved by the *nasya* therapy.

3. Pradana-karma

This is the health maintenance programme. It includes herbo-mineral preparations, nutritional and lifestyle (stress-relieving) advice, as well as advice on yoga and meditation.

Repressed Emotions: According to Ayurveda, toxins that cause disease can be produced by emotional as well as physical factors. For example, fear and anxiety are related to *vatha* and the large intestine. When held inside, these emotions can cause bloating and intestinal pain. Food allergies can also develop because of poor emotional health. Failing to express your emotions can start cravings for foods. This is likely to cause imbalance. Yoga and meditation can help to understand and deal with negative emotions.

RECAP

- According to Ayurveda, each of us has a unique constitution, determined by the balance of three

▶▶

vital energies in the body, known as the three *doshas* or *tridosha*.

- Ayurveds believe that it is essential to detoxify the body before prescribing restorative treatment.
- One of the most effective methods of detoxification is the *purwakarma*, which uses massage techniques and herbal steam therapy to release the toxins.

17

FLUSHING THE KIDNEYS

Our kidneys are perhaps the most important organs of detoxification. They perform many vital functions, one of which is to carry various toxins out of the body in the form of urine. The average amount of urine produced by a human being is about 1.4 litres every day. You can well imagine the tremendous task that our kidneys perform every day of our life, without fail. Kidney failure can result in the build-up of toxins in the body, which can cause death, eventually.

The kidneys keep up a balance of salt and fluid in the body, besides maintaining the right level of acidity. Failure of the kidneys to throw out the toxins from the body can lead to a serious problem known as uraemia. Uraemia occurs due to poisoning caused by accumulation of waste products in the blood.

The inability of the kidneys to excrete toxins can lead to several diseases. We can help them flush out the poisonous waste products by drinking litres and litres of water.

Water therapy

Most of us do not stop to give enough credit to the humble fluid called water. We can survive for quite a few days without food, but without water we will not survive more than a day. Most people think of water as a thirst quencher, but not many realise the curative properties of this simple drink. Water is therapeutic and is the best elixir of life. Not only does it flush out toxins, it prevents heart attacks, cures constipation, prevents cancer and strokes, increases energy levels and gives you a radiant complexion. Water is necessary for our body to operate efficiently. Water is vital to the body in temperature regulation, nerve impulse conduction, circulation, metabolism, immune system, eliminative processes, sensory awareness and perceptive thinking.

Water is the most abundant substance in the human body – on an average, the adult body is 55 to 75 per cent water, or about 10 to 12 gallons of water. The exact amount varies from person to person, depending upon body composition, age and gender. For instance, the leaner you are, the higher proportion of water in your body, because compared with body fat, lean tissue holds more water.

Every body cell, tissue and organ and almost every life-sustaining body process needs water to function. Water regulates your body temperature, keeping it constant at about 98.6° F. Water transports nutrients and oxygen to your body cells and carries waste products away. It moistens tissues in your mouth, eyes and nose, and it softens stools to prevent constipation. It is also the main component of every body fluid such as blood, gastric juice, saliva, amniotic fluid and urine. Water also helps cushion your joints and protects your body organs and tissues.

We use water without realising the benefits we derive from it. Whenever we splash cool water on our tired faces and eyes to refresh them, we are actually using it as a tension remover and refreshing agent. Whenever we soak out tired and weary feet in saline and tepid water, aren't we using it as a pain reliever and healer? A cold water bath on a warm and sweaty day is an instant rejuvenator. Similarly, cold and clear water after a long and hot day's outing is the most refreshing drink, which dissolves away all exhaustion and revitalises us immediately.

Cold-water pads are used to bring down high fever, and hot-water bath is recommended by doctors to remove congestion in the chest and nasal membranes. Hot fomentation can be extremely beneficial in relieving congestion. Steam inhalation is excellent in clearing up the phlegm during common colds. Gargling with hot water and salt can bring relief to sore and aching throats. These are just some of the common hydrotherapy treatments used by most of us without even realising that we are using water as a healer.

Water is the cheapest and best cure for many physical problems. It flushes out the toxins most effectively, ridding the body of many harmful substances that we imbibe each day through the polluted environment and infected food. Just drinking plenty of pure water can dislodge the toxins through urine, faeces and sweat. Water aids in digestion; a person who takes in lots of water can never be constipated.

Seldom do we pause and think about the food we are consuming. In the fast-paced modern life, it is far easier to consume the packaged stuff than the healthy vegetables and fruits. Canned food, preservative-laden packets, rich in chemicals, and fast foods are the order of the day. No one has the time to cook fresh vegetables or sit down to a proper meal. Grabbed sandwiches in the office, gallons of coffee and soft drinks wreak havoc on our system. Is it a wonder that the constipation problem hounds most people of the younger generation? Realisation that the clogged digestive system and toxin build-up can eventually lead to colon cancer and other hazardous diseases seems to rarely hit the busy executives till it is the day of reckoning.

In the recent years a lot of research has gone into water therapy, also known as hydrotherapy. It has been found that hydrotherapy can relieve headaches, hypertension, obesity, eye problems, hyperacidity, and all kinds of digestive disorders, uro-genital diseases as well as diabetes.

Hydrotherapy, or 'water healing' as it is literally translated, is one of the oldest, cheapest and safest methods of treating many common ailments. Both the ancient Greeks and Romans used hot and cold water baths extensively, and many of the modern spas throughout Europe owe their origins to Roman bathing centres. Similarly, the Native Americans were familiar with the use of sweat-lodges for physical and spiritual cleansing, and were proficient in various hydrotherapeutic techniques. In recent centuries, however, some of this knowledge and expertise were lost.

A Bavarian Dominican monk, Sebastian Kneipp, largely revived the therapeutic uses of water in Europe in the nineteenth century. He believed that people had considerable innate healing powers and that water applications were a medium for stimulating or occasionally soothing our recuperative efforts. His ideas have continued to be influential to this day, and in spas in Germany it is possible to experience one of 50 or so different water applications for a variety of ailments.

Typical treatments may include contrast bathing, using alternating baths of hot and cold water. These are usually what are termed sitz baths, a kind of hip bath that immerses the lower trunk, while the feet may be placed in footbaths of contrasting temperature in order to stimulate the circulation. Other forms of treatment may include high-pressure hosing with cold water, hot or cold body wraps, friction rubs, or baths with various ingredients added for extra elimination – for example, mud baths, Epsom salt baths or thalasso-therapy (seawater baths). We instinctively recognise the therapeutic benefits of water in our everyday lives. At home, for example, we take baths and showers not only to cleanse the body but also, after gardening or strenuous exercises, to help relieve fatigue and prevent stiffness.

Cold body wraps are made by soaking a sheet in cold water and wrapping it around the body, then covering this with a dry sheet and blanket. The initial cold is quite quickly replaced by warmth. These wraps are used for a number of conditions such as chronic muscle strains and backache. The sitz baths are often recommended for conditions such as chronic constipation, congestion in the pelvic area, recurrent cystitis and period pains. The sprays have similar effects to the baths, depending on their temperature, but are generally more stimulating to the circulation. A milder effect is achieved by whirlpool baths, which are increasingly popular in homes, gyms and spas.

Some recent medical research has shown the benefits of cool baths for reducing high blood pressure and improving peripheral circulation, and the contrasting applications of hot and cold water compresses and such like have a strong effect on the immune system. So hydrotherapy has very definite physiological effects. As a note of caution, prolonged exposure to very hot water is not a good idea for pregnant women or anyone with hypertension or heart disease, so be careful with saunas, Turkish baths, whirlpools and so on. Regular shorter sessions are often more beneficial.

Apart from going to specialists for hydrotherapy, one can practise simple rules that can be incorporated easily into our lifestyles.

For natural good health and maintenance of impeccable digestion, one needs to drink plenty of water. A minimum of 6–8 glasses is the least one can drink, but an intake of about 10 glasses is more effective in keeping the system in balance and good health. Don't wait to drink water till you feel the dryness in your throat and your brain signals thirst.

It only takes a one per cent fluid loss in the body for it to become dehydrated. This generally happens prior to any conscious sensation of being thirsty. Very small shortages of water can dramatically change and disrupt biochemistry. Exercise physiologists consider water as the single most important variable in peak performance. Your muscles can lose up to 10 per cent of their contractile strength and eight per cent of speed from only three per cent dehydration.

A small change makes a big difference when it comes to water. If you do a lot of travel by air, you can lose as much as two pounds of water in a three to four hour flight. Stress, alcohol and caffeine, all influence the amount of water and the speed in which your body loses it. Any of these factors, alone or in combination, could cause a small but critical shrinkage of the brain. This small shrinkage will impair neuromuscular coordination, decrease concentration and slow down the thinking process. The average amount of water loss per day is two cups through breathing, two cups through invisible perspiration, and six cups through urination and bowel movements. That is a total of 10 cups lost per day without taking into account perspiration from exercise or hard work, excessively dry air, or alcohol and caffeine consumption.

How much water do you need each day?

Most people need between eight and 10 cups of water daily.

You can also sneak in more water through the foods you eat. Foods like lettuce, watermelon, broccoli and grapefruit are more than 90 per cent water. Keep in mind, however, that water needs increase to about 10 to 12 cups per day if you exercise frequently. During a tough workout, the body can lose two litres of fluid per hour through sweat. Athletes should drink six to eight ounces of fluid about 15 minutes before a workout, and then pause regularly during exercise for more. If you are working out for more than an hour, a sports drink will help in replacing lost electrolytes.

Drinking water in less quantity leads to the thickening of blood. What happens when the blood thickens? It doesn't absorb as much oxygen as it should, leading to incomplete oxidation of the blood cells. This in turn leads to lethargy and lack of energy.

The heart is forced to work harder, and the blood vessels are also put under tremendous pressure to pump up the thick blood. As a result, one could suffer from a heart attack or a stroke. The body resistance falls and immunisation system is weakened resulting in easy susceptibility to diseases. A compromised immune system and lowered defences naturally invite all kinds of ailments that are present in the atmosphere.

The healthy and glowing complexion of a well-hydrated person can become the envy of many. No amount of cosmetics or creams can give the healthy radiance that comes with drinking at least 10 glasses of water every day. The skin needs a lot of moisture and that is provided by water that keeps it in a moisturised condition. Since skin also happens to be one of the toxin cleansers of our body, it needs to remain hydrated, so that enough sweating can take place and the toxins are thrown out of the body.

If you are looking for an easy, inexpensive and no-side-effects kind of treatment for health and radiance, water is the panacea. Go ahead and down those litres of elixir that are one of nature's most neglected gifts.

RECAP

- Our kidneys are one of the most important organs of detoxification.
- They perform many vital functions, one of which is to carry various toxins out of the body in the form of urine.
- Failure of kidneys can result in the build-up of toxins in the body, which can cause death, eventually.
- Water therapy is one of the easiest ways to keep the kidneys working at the optimum level.
- Water is therapeutic. It flushes out toxins, prevents heart attacks, cures constipation, prevents cancer and strokes, increases energy levels and gives you a radiant complexion.
- Water is vital to the body in temperature regulation, nerve impulse conduction, circulation, metabolism, immune system, eliminative processes, sensory awareness and perceptive thinking.
- A clogged digestive system and toxin build-up can eventually lead to colon cancer and other hazardous diseases. Water helps eliminate the problem.
- Water flushes out the toxins most effectively. Just drinking plenty of pure water can dislodge the toxins through urine, faeces and sweat.

RECAP

SECTION III

18

LEARNING TO RELAX

Life is a series of constant physical and mental activities. Couple that with emotional necessities, and you have a perfect recipe for a stressful day. The fast pace of life is causing more harm than good. With the 24x7 work culture invading our societies, the number of psychological and neurotic cases is going through the roof. The IT industry is the worst hit, with even the twenty-somethings going through psychological problems. Stress causes a build-up of toxins in the body as well as mind. An accumulation of physical and mental toxins impairs our performance and health. Over a period of time, the toxin build-up can lead to major diseases that can sometimes become fatal.

The body and mind experience true relaxation when little or no energy is consumed. It is nature's way of recharging. It is true that there is very little physical action in the modern life as compared to the past; it is more of mental exhaustion that the present generation is experiencing. Deskbound jobs and ease of travelling have cut down the physical exercise factor. What is not realised is that even mental stress can bunch up the muscles and keep them taut through the day, leading to physical exhaustion.

Haven't you noticed how your jaws are clenched or the facial muscles tightened along with those in the shoulder and back, whenever you are stressed? These muscles can cause much discomfort and pain when they remain in the tense condition for a long time. Headaches, backaches and shoulder aches are just some of the manifestations of bunched-up and tense muscle groups.

Without proper relaxation the body and mind become overworked and inefficient. Exhausted body muscles need relaxation as much as the mind that is seized with anxiety and stress.

The relentless exposure to daily, chronic anxiety is the most toxic form of stress. The body releases certain kinds of chemicals under high stress that can damage the immune system and lead to different kinds of illnesses. Stress can harm neurons in the brain, causing memory problems, hamper sexual performance, and lead to heart attacks. No one is going to believe this, but stress can also make you fat. Digestive disturbances like flatulence, constipation, diarrhoea, acidity and stomach-aches are some of the other symptoms that can occur due to stress. Apart from all these physical problems, there are many psychosomatic and emotional manifestations that are caused by excessive stress.

Stress alters the normal pattern of our brain waves. It agitates the mind. What have brain waves got to do with relaxation? Everything! It is only when you attain a particular brain wave that you are totally relaxed and stress free.

An easy way to understand the brain waves is to compare the four basic brain waves (Delta, Theta, Alpha, Beta) with the four gears on a car. Delta (the slowest wave) is first gear. Theta is second gear. Alpha is third gear, and Beta is the fourth gear. These gears have been provided because driving a car requires different gears to deal with diverse kinds of driving situation; it is not possible to drive by using a single gear. Similarly, no single brain wave is best for all of the challenges of life. We get into trouble if one of the gears on our car goes out, or if we forget to use some of the gears. Continuing the same analogy, imagine the trouble we could get into if we were to use only a single kind of brain wave.

Imagine driving a car, beginning with the first gear, and then shifting directly into fourth gear without bothering to use the second and third gears. Not only will we get low fuel efficiency, but the repair bills will also multiply. The same is true of our brains. Sadly, many people often skip their second and third brain gears – the Theta and Alpha. The penalty for driving our brains in this manner is low productivity and high medical bills.

If you want to feel less stress and anxiety, you should increase the amount of your Alpha waves. This may also improve your immune system, since stress weakens the immune systems. If you want to be more creative, you should learn how to increase the amount of your Alpha waves. Highly creative people have more Alpha brain waves than non-creative people. If you want to have more peak performance in athletic activity, and in other areas of your life, you should learn how to increase the amount of your Alpha waves.

Most of the time we are using Beta waves, which are associated with higher stress, and our day-to-day problem-solving. Relaxed and focused mental activity is associated with Alpha neural signalling. As anxious Beta neural activity decreases, clarity increases in mental activity. Learning occurs in an effortless manner, as learning acquired by exposure to sets of perceived stimuli. While experiencing Alpha, one realises an increased ability to solve problems. Thus, one quickly learns the advantages of existing in a clear perceptual state of mind. However, most of us use the left side of our brain, which happens to be Beta-dominated.

The simple fact is that both Alpha and Theta waves are calming in nature but the Theta waves, being very difficult to attain, remain elusive for most of us. The Alpha wave, however, is easier to attain and one must make an attempt to attain it for at least a couple of hours each day. Whether you do it through meditation or prayers or whatever means is up to you.

A quick entry into the Alpha mode

Although it may take a person quite some time to get into the Alpha brain waves, here is a simple method geared to give you quick result.

Sit in a relaxed position – preferably on the ground in cross-legged position.

Close your eyes and take three deep breaths.

Turn the pupils upwards at an angle of about 22° and begin counting backwards from 100, in your mind.

As you count 100, 99, 98, 97, 96, 95 . . . you will begin to feel calm. By the time you reach the count of 50, you would have attained the Alpha state.

A quick de-stressing technique

Wear loose and comfortable clothes. Lie down on the floor in a quiet and dark room. Place a pillow or cushion under your head and knees. Either let your hands and arms rest by your side or gently upon your stomach, whichever feels the most comfortable.

It is essential that you feel really comfortable. If necessary, use more pillows – perhaps under your feet and forearms.

Start the technique only when you are certain of your comfort because the slightest sense of discomfort can ruin the technique.

Relax and let your mind go blank. Take a couple of deep breaths and sigh the air away.

Now you are ready to start reducing tension in your muscles. The technique involves letting go of all the muscles in the body, starting at the toes, working gradually up the body and ending with the face. To begin, concentrate on your left foot.

Tense all the muscles – curling the toes and scrunching the foot. Hold for a few seconds. Let go, and make them feel floppy, heavy and warm, as if they are sinking in to the pillow. It may take a little practice to perfect this technique, but you will get there after a while.

Move onto the calf muscles on the left leg. Tense the muscles, hold and let go. Feel the heaviness and warmth of the leg and foot.

Apply the same technique on the left thigh. Concentrate on the left leg – does it feel heavy, warm and relaxed? Is it sinking into the floor or bed? If the answers are 'no', tense the whole leg, hold it in tension until it feels difficult to hold the position any longer, then let go completely.

Repeat the same process with the right leg.

When both legs feel heavy and numb, continue moving up the body. Clench your buttocks tightly and let go; pull in your stomach muscles, hold tight, relax; let them fall back towards the spine into the floor or bed. Feel the warmth spreading up your body.

Breathe deeply and evenly a few times, then sigh the breath away; imagine you are sighing all the tension out of your body.

Move on to your left hand, squeeze your hand into a fist, hold tight and let go. Tighten the muscles in the arm and then let them flop. Continue with your right arm. Repeat if the arms are not relaxed and heavy. They should feel numb and impossible to move.

Hunch your shoulders up towards your ears, hold, let go; let them sink into the floor. It may be necessary to repeat this movement a few times as we hold a lot of tension in our shoulders. Pull the shoulders up towards the ceiling and let them flop back into the ground. Repeat a couple of times.

Rock your head gently from side to side in order to loosen the neck. Feel the total relaxation of the body and breathe deeply a few times. Relax, feel the warmth and quiet.

The face is the most difficult part of the body to relax; yawn widely with an open mouth, let go; purse the lips out in a pout, then relax; frown fiercely, let go; move the scalp by raising the eyebrows, then relax.

By now your whole body should feel relaxed. Breathe evenly in and out, saying to yourself with each breath that you feel more and more relaxed, peaceful and warm.

Rest for around 15 minutes. Do not jump up and start racing around. Let yourself come slowly and gently.

Stretch and give yourself a shake before you get immersed in daily grind of your life.

The yogic way

The wise men of ancient India knew the value of yogic exercises and relaxation. They invented different postures of yogic exercises to tone the body and keep it fit. At the same time, they invented the best posture for relaxing the mind and the body. They called it the shavasana – the posture of the dead or the corpse pose.

Shavasana or the corpse pose is a most effective way to de-stress and attain ultimate relaxation. This single asana can help in the management of hypertension, anxiety, exhaustion, insomnia and other stress-related ailments. Yet, it requires no special equipment and is one of the easiest asanas to perform. Its efficacy lies in the fact that it brings the mind to the Alpha state, which is the key to creativity and good health. Shavasana brings about the calm state of mind that is excellent for visualisation and relaxation.

This pose can also be practised any time when one requires a few minutes of total rest and relaxation. All you require is a quiet place and solitude. For greater effectivity one can incorporate a technique that requires the watching of the breathing rhythm or inwardly chanting the mantra of one's choice.

All one has to do is to let the muscles relax, feel the circulation of prana throughout the system and be attuned to cosmic energies. This calms the brain and helps relieve stress and mild depression.

To perform shavasana

Lie flat on your back with the hands resting along the sides. Keep the legs straight and together with the heels touching each other.

Relax all the muscles in the body. Begin with the toes and loosen up the muscles till they become limp. Next, release the muscles of the ankles progressing upwards slowly to the calves and then the thighs. As you traverse through each part of the body, keep relaxing the muscles groups in that area. Loosen up the muscles in the hips, abdomen, heart, the shoulders, neck, arms, elbows and the palm till you reach the fingers. Finally, let the muscles of the head, eyes, lips and ears be relaxed.

By the time you have finished with all the muscles in the body, you will begin to experience a feeling of total relaxation and your breathing will have slowed down to become more regular.

Lie in this pose for about five minutes, turn to the left and count 12, next, turn to the right and count 12. Now get up slowly from your right side.

Initially, you could begin with holding the position for about five minutes and then gradually increase the duration to 15 minutes.

This asana is excellent for hypertension and for bringing down the blood pressure.

In shavasana, we let go of any particular breathing technique and simply allow the breath to move through its inherent inhaling and exhaling pattern. As the breath finds its way through the open channels of the body, the mind does so as well, by weaving itself into the strands of thought and sensation that flow through the body. When the breath is free, the mind is free. When the breath is allowed to move naturally, the mind settles into itself. When the mind relaxes, the tongue and palette become spacious, the roof of the mouth lifts and hollows, and the central core of the body opens up.

RECAP

- Stress causes a build-up of toxins in the body as well as mind. An accumulation of physical and mental toxins impairs our performance and health.
- Over a period of time, the toxin build-up can lead to major diseases that can sometimes become fatal.

▶▶

- Chronic anxiety is the most toxic form of stress. The body releases certain kinds of chemicals under high stress that can damage the immune system.
- Stress can harm neurons in the brain, causing memory problems, hamper sexual performance, and lead to heart attacks.
- The bad news is that stress can also make you fat.
- Stress causes digestive disturbances like flatulence, constipation, diarrhoea, acidity and stomachaches.
- Many psychosomatic and emotional problems are also caused by excessive stress.
- Relaxation is the only antidote of stress. So incorporate some relaxing activities in your daily grind.
- Various methods like shavasana are available for complete relaxation of the body and the mind.

19

ALTERING THE LIFESTYLE

One of the most important ways to detoxify is to alter the lifestyle. If you are a kind who love hamburgers and pizzas downed with gallons of fuzzy aerated drink, spend more time at the desk than outdoors, breathe shallow due to stress, and hate the very idea of working out, you need to examine your lifestyle. You are number one on the hit list as far as toxin accumulation is concerned.

Why do you think most of the newer diseases have been called lifestyle diseases? Simply because they are caused due to unhealthy lifestyle and include diseases like diabetes, hypertension and even cancer.

One classic example of today's philosophy is the phrase 'living life king size'. This suggests that we have only one time around and we had better do it up right because there may be no tomorrow. We gorge on food that is fit to be trashed, party all night, work all day, stimulate our senses with stimulants like coffee, tea or alcohol, load our systems with carbonated drinks, stress ourselves beyond the healthy limits and feel good about it. Not for a minute do we pause to think of the consequences. 'This is living, man! And you only live once', we tell ourselves. We limp slowly off into the sunset after some 20 years of significant debilitation.

Is this what living is all about? Is this the life you visualise for yourself? At this minute you may not even realise what I am talking about, but when you are fifty and the body starts rebelling against the ill-treatment you have heaped on it, you will realise the folly of having lived the king-size life.

Today, lifestyle magazines dictate how we should live, what we should eat and wear. The natural way of living has gone out of fashion. The problems faced by people today have become much more complex than before. Society has become more complicated. Somehow the concept of economic 'success' has replaced the traditional values of human bonding, of communication with nature, of a deep knowledge of life, and of what is important in sustaining life and cultivating wisdom.

Ambition and money have replaced the factors that bring true happiness, and they have done so at the inconceivable expense of the land and the environment that supports life. Technological advancement has been achieved at the expense of culture and the way of life born out of the wisdom of the ages, which, for centuries, supported mankind, high cultural expression, and supreme spiritual life, especially among the people of Asian countries.

Gone is the communion of people with each other, with the animals, the land, plants, trees, mountains, water, and spirits. Gone is the knowledge of invisible things, the greater part of us. How small have we have made ourselves, when we focus only on the seen, the tangible. We see only what is outside, not what is within. We have clearly forgotten to respect and revere nature.

Meanwhile, the very chemicals that are creating cancer, birth defects and deaths, continue to be used on the foods. Lifestyle has become the biggest villain in the modern scenario. The toxins we ingest through wrong foods and stressful life harbour toxic thoughts and emotions, wreak havoc on our health and psyche. Whether it is diabetes, heart problem or psychological problems like depression, the root of almost every other ailment can be traced back to unhealthy lifestyle. Lifestyle is a complete package, a way of life we have adopted. It includes diet and exercise along with other factors. Stress is a deadly foe. It is the biggest toxin generator. Practising calming influences like meditation, imagery and music along with a rigorous change in diet can largely help in controlling stress.

We must not lose sight of the greater, higher path of a natural way of life. The more we study the traditional teachings and ways of life of traditional cultures worldwide, the deeper our understanding of nature becomes. Such a study cultivates a multidimensional understanding of life, as perceived and practised by indigenous peoples everywhere.

These days illnesses are more complex and take more time to heal, due to the introduction of complex chemical pollutants and contaminants, as well as synthetic drugs and medicines, into the environment, our food supplies and our bodies. Before the introduction of all this contamination, manipulation and industrialisation of our foods and the environment took place, the body could heal faster. Now it takes longer for some problems to reverse. A changed lifestyle can speed up the healing in most cases.

We live in a time of traumatic transitions. We bring many unresolved problems, conflicts and addictions into our life without knowing how to handle them. They do not all dissolve automatically just because we start eating brown rice. Appropriate dietary adjustment is essential and effective, but discharge (catharsis) and purification at the spiritual level are also important.

Toxic habits like smoking, drug abuse, alcoholism, perpetual anxiety, lack of exercises, unhealthy diet, all add up to the evil known as lifestyle diseases.

Once again reverting to the analogy of a car and our body, I would draw a few relevant parallels. You may buy a new automobile with no expectation of how long you would like it to last. You perceive threat to your brand new car only in terms of accidents or running out of fuel. With this assumption you may give the car little extra care. As long as it has fuel and oil and water, you may drive it very hard, pushing it beyond the limits of its mechanical resilience.

On the other hand, if you were to buy a car expecting it to last for at least 10–15 years, you are more likely to recognise the fact that abusing it will jeopardise its ultimate lifespan and cause serious mechanical problems necessitating major repairs and expense. In this case you would combine a preventive maintenance programme with prudent driving habits so as to optimise your car's life. The same holds true in the case of our body. We push it too far because we do not take into account the twilight years of our lives.

Alcohol

Although alcohol has been found to be beneficial in moderate doses in certain conditions, the harm caused by heavy drinking far overtakes the benefits in most cases. In advanced researches conducted on the results of chronic heavy drinking it was found to lead to an increased risk of several kinds of cancer like those of mouth, throat, oesophagus, liver, pancreas and rectum. The risk is multiplied if a heavy drinker also happens to be a smoker. Studies also revealed that women are at a far greater cancer threat when compared to men who drink. Even a moderate consumption of alcohol (as few as three drinks a week) by women gives them a higher risk of developing breast cancer.

Some of the neurological complications like 'shakes' and hallucinations are 'withdrawal symptoms' suffered by alcoholics. Severe memory loss of the permanent kind may also be seen in such people.

Heavy drinkers are more likely to suffer from peptic ulcers because a regular drinking habit causes chronic inflammation of the stomach, which in turn causes most alcoholics to lose interest in food. This could lead to deficiency in various vitamin groups. The deficiency may not be immediately noticeable as alcoholics maintain a normal weight sometimes exhibiting an increase in weight because alcohol substitutes itself for carbohydrates in the diet.

Chronic heavy drinking has serious impact on how the body absorbs, uses and stores food. Alcohol is metabolised by the liver, a process that takes precedence over other liver functions and interferes with that organ's effectiveness in processing nutrients. In a chronic heavy drinker, fat is stored in the liver instead of being metabolised efficiently. As a result, the liver grows larger and its ability to metabolise many vitamins and minerals is impaired. Damage to the pancreas, stomach and gastrointestinal tract due to chronic heavy drinking may also hinder the absorption of nutrients.

Problems like weakening of the heart muscles, enlargement of the heart and the reduced efficiency of the pumping action have been linked to the excessive intake of alcohol. Eating a balanced diet may protect a heavy drinker from some of these effects, but not all. Another effect is the nerve damage described as polyneuritis – a tingling in the hands and feet, and cramps in the legs are among the symptoms – which may affect a fifth of all alcoholics.

Vitamin and mineral deficiencies – particularly that of magnesium, calcium, phosphorus, zinc, pyridoxine, thiamine, riboflavin, niacin, folic acid and vitamins A, C and D – have been noted in alcoholics.

Reduced dexterity is another outcome of drinking since alcohol is rapidly absorbed by the body and begins to affect the brain in just 10 minutes. The brain could become fuzzy and the coordination of hand and eye begins to fail. Driving becomes difficult as the ability to judge distance becomes impaired. Drinking is also an important cause of accidents and violence both at work and home.

However, these physical and mental effects are complications of alcohol misuse and generally arise only years after the sufferer's personal, social and professional lives have been destroyed.

The peculiar nature of alcoholism is that it starts as a pleasure. From the 'feel-good' stage, it can quickly reach the addiction level if not controlled. Occasional drinking, because it relaxes tensions, frequently becomes 'relief' drinking. The difference between a healthy drinker and a problem drinker is the element of compulsiveness.

Smoking

Smoking adds more toxins to the body than people realise. The link between smoking and lung cancer has been established long ago. Cancer is a disease in which the cells that make up some part of the body multiply wildly without any control. The early warning sign of cancer of the larynx is the persistent cough or a change in the quality of the voice. In the case of lung cancer, the sufferer may spit up blood while coughing or develop a severe pain in the chest.

Chronic bronchitis begins as a smoker's cough, clearing from the air passages of the throat and lungs a slimy mucus produced by the irritating smoke that eventually starts to clog the lungs themselves.

The other problems caused by smoking are severe heart and blood vessel diseases, which kill thousands of people each year. Smoking can also cause sexual dysfunction and psychiatric disorders like depression.

Most people develop nicotine dependency on smoking regularly. It is this dependency which creates withdrawal symptoms when the smokers try to quit smoking.

When you quit smoking

You will feel better, smell better, sleep better and breathe easier. You will cough less and have fewer headaches, stomachaches and respiratory infections. The level of oxygen-depleting carbon monoxide in your blood will decline right away, and your stamina will increase. You will feel less guilty and, of course, you will have more money in your pocket.

In addition to these immediate payoffs, quitting smoking now – no matter what your age is or how long you've been smoking – will give you a number of long-term benefits.

Your heart disease risk starts declining within a year of quitting. After 10–15 years of not smoking, your chances of having a heart attack will be the same as those of the general population.

Your risk of developing lung cancer also begins to decrease within a year. After two years of not smoking, your likelihood of getting lung cancer will decline by almost a third. And after 10–15 years, your lung cancer risk will be almost normal.

Your risk of all health problems related to smoking will decline steadily for 15 years. Then your risk of dying will return nearly to that of someone who has never smoked.

If you are pregnant and quit before the fourth month, your baby is likely to have a higher birth weight than a smoking mother's infant. If you stay off cigarettes, your risk of having a low-birth-weight baby in your next pregnancy will be the same as that of a non-smoker.

Tobacco facts

There are over 4000 compounds in tobacco, 40 of these substances including benzopyrene, nitrosamines, vinyl chloride, arsenic, chromium and nickel are known to be carcinogenic compounds.

500 gaseous compounds including nitrogen, carbon monoxide, ammonia, hydrogen cyanide and benzene have been identified in the volatile phase, which account for about 95 per cent of the weight of cigarette smoke. The other five per cent is particulate.

Tobacco contains a highly poisonous alkaloid called nicotine.

Tobacco kills nearly 10,000 people daily, i.e. one person in every 10 seconds.

Around 35 lakh people die every year, of which 10 lakh are in developing countries.

Tobacco is the cause for 20 per cent of all deaths in developing countries.

Predicted deaths due to tobacco by the year 2020 will be more than the ones caused by HIV, TB, maternal mortality, motor accidents, suicides and homicide combined.

Cancers

This table has been specifically included in the book for the benefit of people who lead a high-risk lifestyle so that they can evaluate their risk levels.

Some cancer risk factors, such as smoking and sun exposure are controllable; others, like age and gender aren't. Regular

Cancer type	Risk factors
Breast	Family history of breast cancer, obesity, late childbearing, and childlessness.
Bladder	Smoking (nearly half of cases), bladder cancer is more common in men than in women.
Cervical	First intercourse at an early age, multiple sexual partners, smoking, history of genital herpes.
Colorectal	Being over 50 with colon polyps or ulcerative colitis; a family history of these disorders or of colon cancer; a high-fat, low-fibre diet.
Leukaemia	Exposure to radiation,benzene and other chemicals.
Lung	Smoking (83 per cent of cases), exposure to asbestos, radiation, and passive tobacco smoke.
Lymphoma	Being over 50, no other known risk factors.
Oral	Smoking, chewing tobacco and heavy alcohol use.
Pancreatic	Smoking, high-fat diet.
Prostate	Risk increases with age, more than 80 per cent of cases occur after 65.
Skin	Fair skin, severe sunburn in childhood, frequent sun exposure and family history of skin cancer.
Uterine	Being postmenopausal with a history of infertility, ovulation failure or abnormal bleeding; also obesity, hypertension, diabetes.

checkups, self-examination of the breasts and skin, and faecal occult blood tests, Pap smears and mammograms are important early detection measures which could prevent many cancer deaths every year.

Some known factors that can be hazardous to health, and are controllable, are: smoking, alcohol and drug abuse, and obesity.

The panacea to most ills is an alteration in the lifestyle, which requires healthy eating habits, regular exercise, a few moments of meditation and no addictions. Even small steps towards a healthier lifestyle can prove immensely rewarding. When you start a new exercise programme, for instance, you may well find that your appetite is more easily regulated, and that you have less desire to smoke or drink (if these are problems for you). Regularly practising a relaxation technique too, though it may take only a few minutes each day, will reduce the need for stimulants, encourage better sleep and, by releasing the energy locked up in stress, increase your vitality.

By now you must have realised the impact that nutrition and lifestyle can make upon your health, and you have also been sensitised to some of the variables which you can adjust to frame a healthier lifestyle.

The first thing that matters is the realisation that the lifestyle you are following is not really the best. Once you have realised that, you have to follow it up with a conviction that you have to do something about it. Now the question is: Where do you begin and how you do it?

Once we have convinced ourselves that we are ultimately responsible for our own state of health, we are ready to explore our own lifestyle. Before that, one must know that a change in lifestyle alone does not guarantee that you will never be ill. All it guarantees is that you will be far healthier than you presently are.

To assess your lifestyle, make a checklist which includes the following areas:

Diet
Stress levels
Leisure
Emotional involvement in eating
The workplace environment
Level of intellectual stimulation

Armed with the checklists, you can easily identify the areas of improvement and work on them. Now that you have made a proper evaluation of your existing lifestyle, it is time to move towards a healthier one. By now you have realised where your strengths and deficiencies lie, and it is time to make the changes and the positive reinforcements which encourage you to continue the change.

Any change that you make in your lifestyle which is designed to better your health will lead you closer to making many other changes. If you start eating better, it will not be too long until you start wanting to exercise or vice versa. The philosophical change that comes from making a commitment to your own health is the most important facet of the programme. The first corner you must turn, which is the largest corner, is to commit yourself to your own responsibility. Then you must design your environment to support the allocation of time to activities which you know are in your best interest and to minimise the time spent on activities which are well recognised as undermining your health. Your body knows how to eat right and live in a healthy way if you would only get out of its way.

When you know where the problem lies, it becomes so much easier to handle it. I bet you are in for a few shocks yourself when you read and evaluate your logs. You must never have really known what kind of food you are consuming, what your daily activities are like and how much time you spend doing things you like in your spare time. It is like a whole new world has opened up before your eyes and you know exactly what you must do.

You do not need to become a nutrition nut and suddenly switch to lentils, tofu and soya as your main source of calories. Prudent dietary selection when you shop for food items can make a tremendous difference in the quality of nutrition. Try to use fundamental starting material as much as possible, such as whole grains, vegetables, legumes and brown rice. Similarly, when you find that your activity log shows hardly any activity, you could start by introducing some nice calorie-burning activity. Or for that matter, if the leisure log indicates a complete vacuum in terms of hobbies, maybe its time to pick a challenging and satisfying one. Maybe you have some secret talents, which need to be nurtured, but you never found time or inclination to do so. Now is the time to do it.

Nothing will happen overnight, remember you have taken some 30–40 years to develop these habits, whether food or activities. Changing them will come with time. But a slow commitment to a change in philosophy will help everyone to turn the corner and become friends again with their own bodies, working jointly toward optimising health and minimising the need for crisis medical intervention.

RECAP

- ➥ One of the most important ways to detoxify is to alter the lifestyle.
- ➥ Lifestyle has become the biggest villain in the modern scenario. The toxins we ingest through

▶▶

wrong foods and stressful life harbour toxic thoughts and emotions and wreak havoc on our health and psyche.

- Whether it is diabetes, heart problem or psychological problems like depression, the root of almost every other ailment can be traced back to unhealthy lifestyle.
- Lifestyle is a complete package that largely involves diet and exercise along with mind control. Stress is a deadly foe. It is the biggest toxin generator.
- Toxic habits like smoking, drug abuse, alcoholism, perpetual anxiety, lack of exercises, unhealthy diet, all add up to the evil known as lifestyle diseases.
- Smoking adds more toxins to the body than people realise. The link between smoking and lung cancer has been established long ago.
- Chronic heavy drinking is linked with an increased risk of cancer of the mouth, throat, oesophagus, liver, pancreas and rectum. The risk is heightened if a heavy drinker is also a smoker.
- The panacea to most ills is an alteration in the lifestyle, which requires healthy eating habits, regular exercise, a few moments of meditation and no addictions.
- Even small steps towards a healthier lifestyle can prove immensely rewarding.

20

DETOXIFYING THE MIND

Mind is the strongest thing God has given man. Using it the right way can make all the difference between joy and sorrow; success and failure. The only difference between a successful man and an unsuccessful one is the ability of the former to harness all mental energies in a positive manner.

Physical power is not the ultimate form of power. This has been demonstrated again and again in the stories of triumph told by survivors of horrible crimes and abuse. Victor Frankl, author of *Man's Search for Meaning*, describes how holocaust victims used the power of their mind to survive unscathed. Although they were physically defeated, they still had the power to choose their response.

Is mental strength more important than the physical one? Somebody asked me the other day, and I answered, 'Yes. It is more important to have a strong mind than to possess a powerful body because a strong body without a strong mind is of no use. Yet, a strong mind with a weak body can still function quite remarkably.'

Remember the story of David and Goliath? Wasn't Goliath much bigger and physically stronger than David? Yet, David could slay the giant without any problems because he was mentally strong. Mind is all-powerful and potent. It gives us the direction to head in the right path, when used well.

The mind–body connection is no longer a myth to be used by godmen and spiritual leaders only. It is a connection that is recognised and respected by doctors and surgeons as well. The mental toxins accumulated over a period of time can play havoc with the physical wellness of a person. We heap various toxic thoughts on the mind and expect to remain healthy. That is quite impossible. Most of us live in the past, regretting the things we have done, the things people have done to us or lamenting what could have been. We live in a state of constant anxiety and fear, wearing ourselves down till we fall a prey to hypertension and other diseases.

Strong passions and negative emotions cause chemical changes in the body, generating poisonous substances, which are injurious and fatal to healthy growth. Internally-generated concerns like regret, repentance and guilt can lead to severe depression.

Did you know that arthritis could be caused by broken marriages, worries, anxieties, financial problems and holding on to past resentments?

Anxiety is another name for fear, which also includes worry and panic. It arises in uncertain situations, when the prospect of danger lingers, and the result is an urge to escape or, if that is not possible, to fight. The body undergoes a transformation from a state of calm to a state of alarm. The heart and lungs work faster, and muscles tighten. When this response goes on for too long, the effects are painful and damaging.

Sigmund Freud, the founder of psychoanalysis, showed that anxiety is a fundamental emotion that influences our lives from earliest childhood.

Anxiety occurs where you are concerned that circumstances are out of control. In some cases, being anxious and worrying over a problem may generate a solution. Normally it will just result in negative thinking.

There are five major desires that cause anxiety; most of them are unrealistic, of course. Here they are:

The need to have the love and admiration of all people important to you, all the time. This is unrealistic because you have no control over other people's minds. They can have bad days, see things in odd ways, make mistakes or can be plain disagreeable and awkward.

The need to be thoroughly competent at all times. This is unrealistic because you only achieve competence at a new level by making mistakes. Everybody has bad days and everybody makes mistakes.

The belief that external factors cause all misfortune. Often negative events can be caused by your own negative attitudes. Similarly, your own negative attitudes can cause you to view neutral events negatively. Someone else might find something positive in something you view as a problem.

The desire that events should always turn out the way that you want them to and that people should always do what you want is the cause for most anxieties. Other people have their own agendas and do what they want to do.

The belief that past bad experience will inevitably control what will happen in the future. You can very often improve or change things if you try hard enough or look at things in a different way.

To be able to control these beliefs means to have a grip over anxiety.

What could have been

The Yin and Yang of life guarantees that there will be ups as well as downs in life. This is probably a very good thing;

otherwise, the ups would not be fully appreciated. If one lives with the philosophy that life will eventually balance things out, it becomes easier to deal with the lows of life. How to practise that philosophy is all up to the mind.

'Learn from the past, plan for the future, but live in the present,' said wise men, and the words remain true to this day.

Although many of us are aware of the wisdom of living in the present, how we love to hold on to the past! We tend to hold on to our memories and the ones that are dear to us are the ones that are painful. We nurture them like babies, cherish those painful moments and bring them up in the mind repeatedly and sadistically. We brood and tend to them because we don't want to part with them. These unhappy memories interfere with our present state of mind and happiness.

When unpleasant memories refuse to rest, they sit like landmines in the recesses of consciousness waiting to be triggered by a casual thought or association. The painful memories that return to haunt us are usually the experiences that were never resolved, like unfinished business and unsaid good-byes. Regret, resentment and grudges chain us to things we cannot change.

Peace with the past does not necessarily mean finding resolution. It means accepting things that happened just the way they happened.

'The stories that you tell about your past shape your future.'

—Eric Ransdell

Life is all about moving on, to forget what happened in the past and go on. Even if the past was very happy, don't allow it to become the measure for your future. Take each day as it comes, live it to the hilt and do your best.

Like Deepak Chopra says, 'The past is history and the future is a mystery. It is the present which is a gift from God.'

Much of our toxic thoughts and restlessness of the mind are due to the habit of clinging to the past. The moment we decide to step out of it and walk into the present, we would have gained control over mental toxicity, to a large extent.

RECAP

- Did you know that arthritis could be caused by broken marriages, worries, anxieties, financial problems and holding on to past resentments?
- The mental toxins accumulated over a period of time can play havoc with the physical wellness of a person.
- We heap various toxic thoughts on the mind and expect to remain healthy. That is quite impossible.
- Most of us live in the past, regretting the things we have done, the things people have done to us or lamenting what could have been.
- We live in a state of constant anxiety and fear wearing ourselves down till we fall a prey to hypertension and other diseases.

21

TOXIC THOUGHTS

'All that we are is the result of our thoughts; the world is made up of our thoughts.'

—Gautama Buddha

Thoughts can be toxic. They can act as a poison in our body system. We can toxify our minds with negative thoughts, in much the same manner as we toxify our bodies with junk food. Last year, I happened to attend a health camp. Apart from the usual health lectures, there was an interesting seminar that dealt with the toxicity of mind at length. I was quite impressed by the lecture. One particular piece of information that I carried back home was that our mind has the capacity to process approximately 92,000 thoughts per day, and according to the self-development expert, our lives would be significantly enhanced, if at least three of these thoughts were positive, and self-affirming. Now, that was something to think about!

Till then, I had assumed that toxic-thoughts syndrome was solely my own personal demon. However, after attending the camp I was convinced that it is an international phenomenon that has no respect for age, image, gender, race or national origin. Certainly, the reportedly self-destructive behaviour of super model Naomi Campbell, and even the widely-reported low self-esteem of Princess Diana give credence to the universality of 'negative thinking'. At some point in our lives, statistics reveal that even the most accomplished and apparently self-confident persons experience the debilitating effects of 'toxic thoughts' syndrome. Oprah Winfrey, for example, admits, 'I have struggled with my own self-value for many, many years.' Even when she was winning numerous awards and public applause, Oprah said she was 'filled with self-doubt and fear of not being good enough!'

The good news is that we can transcend our tendency to lament our lot, belittle our achievements, question our competence and doubt our ability.

Some life-changing maxims for transforming our thought processes that could help are:

Accentuate the positive. Become your own personal champion. Remember that most of the unhappiness comes from comparing your weaknesses to someone else's strength. You are as great as you think you are!

Discover the path to positivity. It can dynamise your life and alter the entire script unbelievably.

Create your own healing experiences. Make an appointment with yourself for pampering, and reminiscing over your previous successes. Your accomplishments are as real as your perceived failures.

Lighten the burden. Perhaps your expectations are too high. Give yourself permission to let go. Quit trying to be perfect. You're ok just as you are.

Most importantly, pat yourself on the back for the strides that you've made, and take life one day at a time. This is not a dress rehearsal for the real thing. Therefore, we should live on our own terms, minus toxic thoughts.

Basically, toxic thoughts are a form of stress and that stress interferes with the transmission of intelligence over the nerve system. Very simply, I can talk to people and get them to recall a stressful event in their life and at the same time measure their blood pressure. What do you think happens to their blood pressure as they recall a stressful event? The blood pressure would go up; their heart rate would go up; and respirations would go up. These are just a few noticeable conditions; what happens internally in the body cells can hardly be observed.

As long as we remove as much of that toxic stress as we can, the body systems will be allowed to work unencumbered.

What generates toxic thoughts?

Certain characteristics generate toxic thoughts more than others. Perfectionists, control freaks, chronic worriers and doomsday predictors excel in harbouring toxic thoughts more than those who are easy going, friendly and optimistic.

Perfectionists are a highly stressed lot. In their drive for perfection, they bulldoze through the imperfections of the world, and everyone knows that the world is more imperfect than perfect. Perhaps the perfectionist realises that the imperfections will come his way but refuses to believe it. In their minds they equate imperfections with failure. The fear of failure generates toxic pattern of thoughts.

For the control freaks it is a different ball game altogether. When we try to exercise excessive control on people and situations, we begin to take the responsibility of things beyond our control. We take the accountability for the resultant events, which are totally out of our power. The fact is that no one has any control on anything but himself or herself. The remorse and guilt felt by the control freak for situations that are beyond control generates toxic thought process.

Chronic worrier has the ability to worry about things that may not be on the horizon for the next one century. He worries about the doomsday, the nuclear proliferation, the growing environmental hazards and impending wars. Not that it is wrong to think about these events, but the worrier excels in producing vividly-coloured images of the unforeseen events and allows them to disturb the mind. He literally takes the responsibility of worrying about things that may never happen. In his mind, thoughts like 'I can never find a suitable job', 'I will never find happiness', and 'The world is doomed' find frequent incursion.

The regretter is always a step behind the worrier. He regrets and rues all the things that have passed him by. While the worrier is worried about the future events, the regretter worries and regrets the past events. Either way, the two excel in generating toxic thoughts.

Toxic thought pattern cannot be wiped out in a day because they are the result of many years. But they can be replaced slowly and gradually by positive thought process.

Cleansing toxic thoughts

The mind is the most restless thing on the earth. It runs like an unbridled horse from one thought to the other before we can catch our breath and say 'stop'. You will know what I am talking about if you have ever tried to harness your mind and meditate for a few minutes. When you understand that mind governs the body, then you begin to give more power to the mind. Thoughts have to be understood and applied in the right manner, before they become effective. They come to us in crude forms. That is why people who try to handle crude thoughts without reasoning get no result and say that thoughts are not effective.

Because thoughts can't be seen and have no physical substance, many people assume they are without power and effect. However, since recorded time, we have been cautioned and directed by astute philosophical and spiritual teachers such as Plato, Christ and Buddha that what we focus upon eventually becomes part of our existence.

This concept, once dismissed as religious or superstitious bunkum, is now being proven by scientific research undertaken by quantum physics and neurobiology. Computational neuroscience is a new concept, which tries to fathom the working of the brain and makes an effort to understand the impulses that are generated by it.

Our mind, body and spirit make an extremely sensitive, intricately balanced and interconnected system, and they need to be harmonised for optimum health. With time we have attained awareness about bodily health and try to balance our diets by eating nutritious foods and taking dietary supplements, but few pay attention to mental hygiene, which incidentally is one of the essential building blocks of a healthy, balanced life.

Negative, angry, sad and self-defacing thoughts are toxic to our system. By harbouring them we are literally pouring poisonous elements into our body. These poisons activate neuro-physiological responses within the body and, when combined with other causative factors, lead to the appearance of diseases such as cancer, allergies, immune deficiencies, headaches and colitis. Mental toxicity can cause depression, anxiety, worry and a sense of hopelessness within the soul.

Whenever we are assailed by unpleasant or negative situations in our lives, we tend to look for external causes of these happenings. We use excuses and blame others for what we experience. However, situations, events or people do not determine our moods or feelings. You can be as happy as you allow yourself to be. No one and no situation can make you unhappy if you don't allow them to do so. The way you think or perceive a situation will direct your feelings and moods about it. How and what you think has a profound impact upon your physical, emotional and spiritual well-being.

Toxic thought patterns lead to various forms of self-destructive behaviour, including the creation and retention of regrets that burden us. Letting go of our regrets and overcoming the anger, pain and guilt they feed requires us to identify the toxic thought patterns that support them. Writing journals, spoken or written affirmations, creative visualisations, prayer, meditation, thought analysis and sharing them with others are among the spiritual and psychological tools we can use to counter toxic thought patterns.

Our ability to think can be a blessing or a curse, so we can always choose to bless ourselves. Thinking is a habit, a learned response. These learned responses are imbibed right from the day we were born and are highly influenced by our growing-up surroundings. These influences continue to affect us till we die. Like any habit or behaviour, thinking patterns and tendencies can be unlearned or changed if one is motivated. It is like deciding to stop smoking. Making a conscious decision to alter your habits and thought patterns will have a direct impact on what you experience.

If you are in the habit of using phrases like 'why me', 'poor me', 'it always happens to me', 'I never get a break', or any other negative thought patterns, you need to break the habit. Replace them with positive affirmation.

We do not have a choice in the matter of our time or place of birth, nor can we choose our parents and situations. We are helplessly choice-less in the matter of death also. What we have a choice about is the way we live. We can choose to live with optimism and positivity. We have the choice to clean our minds of negative emotions and thoughts. Simply by exercising these options we can make an immense impact on our life. A simple cleansing of the mind can be the first step towards a happy living.

Easier said than done, it takes immense self-control to work your way out of the trap. Try the following steps to detoxify your thinking and move towards good mental hygiene:

Purge the Thought: Most of us are unable to achieve what we set out to achieve only because of the 'I can't' thoughts that cloud our vision. Opt to empower yourself. Use your visualisation ability to reaffirm the 'I can' thoughts. Henry Ford once said, 'Whether you think you can't or whether you think you can, you're right.'

Switch the Thought: Each time you realise that you are using the negative thought, replace it with a positive one. Shake your head, tap it with the knuckles and reinforce the replacement. We have an inherent ability to pick the thoughts of our choice. Use this ability to choose your thoughts and your feelings will follow. Create a resource of positive affirmations like 'I am strong and capable' and positive images, like a superman, to replace the negative ones. When you become aware of an uncomfortable feeling or thought, intercept it with the affirmation or image.

Review the Validity: Review the thoughts to examine their validity. Ask yourself, 'Is this right?' 'Does the situation justify such negative thoughts?' and 'Is the thought realistic?' Most of the time you will find that your thought process will alter from the negative to the positive.

The Right to Be Joyful: Focus on your right to be happy rather than your justification to be angry or sad. Holding on to anger or sadness only weakens you. It's a choice you deliberately make.

Rephrase and Reject: Reform each thought in terms of what you want in your life rather than what you don't want. For example, thoughts of affluence become 'I want to be well-off' as opposed to 'I don't want to be poor'.

Stop Worrying: Examine the situation objectively. Determine what you can do to influence a positive outcome in the situation and act on it. Anything that you can't do means that you have no influence, and worrying won't change that. When the situation comes to mind, remind yourself of the actions you took, then change your thoughts to create a positive outcome.

Mental Hygiene: Just as we take our daily bath and follow certain rules for physical hygiene, we need to reinforce the rules of mental hygiene. All it takes is a couple of moments a few times every day to repeat an empowering affirmation or review a positive image. This is a boost to your immune system, a mood lifter and a spiritual reconnection.

Using Spirituality: Use your spiritual or religious beliefs to your advantage. Within these frameworks exist beliefs or practices to provide strength and encouragement. For example, 'What you focus on expands', or 'The Lord helps those who help themselves'. Belief is a very powerful motivator that will help to shape your thoughts. Therefore, foster positive and empowering beliefs.

Take Responsibility: It is important for us to take the responsibility for our reactions to events and stop blaming others or situations. You may not have directly been responsible for an event, but you can choose how you react to it. This approach will awaken you to your ability to alter the effects of the situation and not feel helpless and victimised.

Healthy Thoughts: Your body lives out your thoughts. Whether you are experiencing a temporary or long-term illness, focus on all of the healthy, supporting systems of your body. Your body is composed of billions of cells, and out of these most are doing their jobs well. If you are well then express gratitude to your body.

The De-Stress Routine: Take time to de-stress daily. Even a couple of ten-minute breaks in the course of the day can have enormous benefits to your mind and body. Deep breathing, short meditations or regular stretching will relax the nervous system, slow down responses, calm the mind and put you back in touch with your body.

RECAP

- When unpleasant memories refuse to rest, they sit like landmines in the recesses of consciousness, waiting to be triggered by a casual thought or association.
- Painful memories that return to haunt one are usually the experiences that were never resolved, like unfinished business and unsaid good-byes.
- Regret, resentment and grudges chain us to things we cannot change.
- Thoughts can be toxic. They can act as a poison in our body system.
- We can toxify our minds with negative thoughts, in much the same manner as we toxify our bodies with junk food.

22

TOXIC STRESS

Do you sometimes overreact to stressful situations? If so, consider this: A growing scientific consensus is linking abnormal levels of the so-called stress hormone, cortisol, with early childhood experiences that might be considered traumatic. In adults with poor coping skills, cortisol levels rise under minimal stress.

High cortisol has also been associated with heart disease and diabetes in adults and asthma in children.

Increasingly, scientists agree that people suffering from mental illness or eating disorders display similar patterns in the rise and fall of cortisol, which is also associated with a host of other stress-related dangers.

For instance, studies on rats have shown that elevated cortisol increases appetite and boosts abdominal fat, a risk factor for heart disease. The rats also ate during periods they were normally inactive, a factor that further increases the risk of obesity. High levels of cortisol are also associated with chronic psychological stress, which, over time, can block short-term memory. Too much cortisol can kill brain cells, high cortisol has even been shown to raise the risk of heart attack, trigger asthma in children and diabetes in adults.

While controlled stress is often seen as a good thing, the uncontrolled levels can become highly toxic both to the body and mind. The fact that psychological stress can trigger or alter the course of illness has long been apparent. Emotions obviously can affect the autonomic nervous system, and secondarily, heart rate, sweating, and bowel peristalsis (wavelike movement resulting from the contraction and relaxation of muscles in the walls of the digestive tract).

Stress reactions reduce the immunity levels and resistance to infections and diseases. They can alter the heart rate and affect the blood pressure. When confronted with a stressful situation, the human body reacts with a chain of bio-chemical reactions that can affect the entire system. Research shows that stress may cause many diseases, ranging from cardio-vascular irregularities, digestive disorders, menstrual problems, neck and back spasms, headaches, skin disorders, acne, dark circles around the eyes, sleeping disabilities to insomnia. Recent research has also pointed to a low fertility levels in women who are constantly tense.

Each individual has his own tolerance level and the combating arsenal to fight the stress up to a certain extent. Although many people find stress stimulating them to a better performance, stress is a silent killer.

There are several methods of stress control like meditation, *tai chi*, pranayama, praying, self-hypnotism, affirmation, etc. It is imperative to opt for a method that one finds a comfort level with, because it will have to be practised regularly. Elsewhere in the book, various methods of stress management are given, and you can choose the one that you find suitable.

RECAP

- Uncontrolled levels of stress can become highly toxic both to the body and mind.
- Cortisol, the stress hormone, is associated with a host of stress-related dangers.
- Levels of cortisol may depend on early childhood experiences. In adults with poor coping skills, cortisol levels rise under minimal stress.
- Stress reactions reduce the immunity levels and resistance to infections and diseases.
- They can alter the heart rate and affect the blood pressure.

SECTION IV

23

TOXIC NOISE

Does the thought that noise could be toxic amuse you? The truth is that constant exposure to high-decibel noise can impair the hearing and cause other problems like stress, high blood pressure and irritability. Physicians in the urban areas have reported a significant increase in the cases of tinnitus or a ringing sound within the ears even when there is no noise in the surrounding. According to experts, Noise Induced Hearing Loss (NIHL) is gradually becoming an urban phenomenon. Given the growing number of sources of noise and constant exposure to it, people are at the risk of becoming deaf from all that noise. In fact, chronic noise is becoming the bane of urban living.

Most of the time hearing loss results from long-term exposure to less intense sounds. Noises heard close up are more harmful than noises at a distance, and noises at night are often more harmful than noises heard during the day, because we're trying to rest at night.

Because noise often does not produce visible effects, and because there is usually not a distinct cause-and-effect ('dose-response' in medical terms) relationship between a single noise event and a clear adverse health effect, some people believe noise does not pose a serious risk to human health.

But evidence from a number of recent studies, especially on children, provides ample proof that noise harms human health and decreases quality of life.

Apart from being an irritant and stressor, chronic noise can also cause mental distress, ulcers, migraines, acidity, non-cooperative behaviour, aggression, learning impairment, and even contribute to musculo-skeletal and heart problems. Continual exposure to loud noise causes disorder in the endocrinological systems as well as an alteration of the brain biochemistry. The resultant pressure on the autonomic nervous system goes up leading to irritability, anger and sadness, insomnia, depression, besides increased heart rate and hypertension. Continual low-level noise can be also act as a stressor.

A chronic noisy environment leads to poor academic performance in children. In addition, there are the problems of social adjustment. In an interesting study it was found that children who lived in high-noise areas are more violent and aggressive. Another study revealed that children residing near airports, railway stations or high-traffic areas tend to have poorer reading skills. Dr Gary Evans, Psychologist and Environmental Stress specialist at Cornell University, conducted several tests on the harmful effects of toxic noise. One of the tests conducted on children living in noisy areas revealed that the children experienced higher overnight levels of the cortisol, which is a stress-hormone. Stress tests conducted on them showed that their blood pressure was slightly higher than normal, and so were the rate of heartbeats. Prolonged exposure to loud noise leads to fatigue and low energy levels.

Given the fact that the traffic has gone up by leaps and bounds in the recent years and the noise factors have jumped in tandem, more and more people are developing problems of hearing by the age of 60. Add to that the noise of generators, power tools, machinery, loudspeakers, firecrackers and you have a perfect scenario for developing deafness.

Loud music in the discotheques and pubs cause more stress and problems than drinking. Research has found that musicians and DJs in pubs and clubs, who perform regularly in high decibel levels, are prone to NIHL due to continuous exposure to loud noise.

According to a leading ENT specialist, eight hours of exposure to 85dB noise on a daily basis can begin to damage your ears over a period of time. The current fad of listening to music on stereo headsets could be damaging to the ears if the decibels are 110 or higher. Rock concerts where the music is at 120dB can be equally harmful. A jet taking off can sound as loud as 150dB if your house is directly under its flight path. Some people are prone to hearing damage from the sound of firing which occurs between 140 to 170dB. Children who lived in terror-stricken areas or war zones where the constant sound of gun battle hit the eardrums were more likely to suffer from impaired hearing on attaining adulthood. Factory workers in high-noise zones were equally vulnerable to hearing damage. Any sort of sudden, loud noise is likely to cause a temporary loss of hearing, and it can take up to two to three weeks' time for recovery.

A recent research undertaken by Australian scientists brought out shocking facts about the use of iPods, which have become a current craze amongst the younger generation. A quarter of all users of personal digital music players are risking permanent hearing damage by playing them too loud, scientists warn. The study warns that one in four iPod users could become deaf if they don't keep the volume down. They are also vulnerable to tinnitus. Previous studies have shown that extended exposure to volumes of 80dB, roughly equivalent to someone shouting in your ear, can begin to damage the thousands of tiny hair cells that line the inner ear, causing temporary tinnitus.

A study by the National Acoustic Laboratory, Australia, showed that many users of personal music players raise the volume of their players to 105dB – a level that can cause permanent damage if listened to for more than an hour a day. With the advent of iPods in the market, the storing capacity and the resultant playtime have increased tremendously. Some players can store entire CD collections and operate for up to 18 hours on a single battery charge. Graham Frost, chairman of the British Society of Audiology, warned that the large capacities of the personal stereos encouraged long use, thus leading to more damage.

Apart from music, the simple act of driving can lead to an exposure to dangerous levels of noise. Driving through congested areas where the drivers are constantly using their horns raises stress levels as well as tempers. Workplace noise is a major factor of concern amongst experts. Open-area office space where people are exposed to usual office din like noise generated from the fax machines, printers, phones, mobiles was sufficient to accelerate adrenalin levels in the employees. These generated higher stress levels and affected the performance of the staff.

Factory workers who were exposed to toxic noise suffered from sleep-related problems, high anxiety levels, impaired digestion, higher frustration level and irritability.

Awareness that noise can generate enough damage could help in reducing the levels of decibels we suffer in the environment.

RECAP

- Constant exposure to high-decibel noise can impair the hearing and cause other problems like stress, high blood pressure and irritability.
- Chronic noise causes mental distress, ulcers, migraines, acidity, non-cooperative behaviour, aggression, learning impairment, and even contributes to musculo-skeletal and heart problems.
- Continual exposure to loud noise causes disorder in the endocrinological systems as well as an alteration of the brain biochemistry. The resultant pressure on the autonomic nervous system goes up leading to irritability, anger and sadness, insomnia, depression, besides increased heart rate and hypertension.
- Continuous low-level noise can also act as a stressor.

24

TOXIC RELATIONSHIPS

Relationships are the greatest support system for detoxification of the mind. They provide emotional stability and an anchor to our lives. Ask anyone who is assailed with self-doubt, and he will tell you that he lacks the pep talk and confidence-boosting support of relationships.

According to Neal Donald Walsch, 'Relationships are how we relate to others. We have a relationship with everyone we know who is close to us. Relationships are not reserved for our family or someone we are involved with. Each and every interaction we have with another person is the act of relating.'

Most of us spend hours at work but refuse to work on relationships. This is the prime reason for the growing psychological problems in the developed countries. You may surround yourself with all kinds of costly gadget and luxuries, but they won't compensate for human beings. They can't bring warmth to your life, or love for that matter.

One of the ills of modern living, apart from stress, is loneliness. The curse of loneliness can be extremely depressing for most people. With our busy lives, we have built steel walls around ourselves which keep others away. In the past, people were not equipped with televisions or modern trappings of VCD, etc. So they spent time communicating with people and enjoyed pastimes, which promoted togetherness. As a result, the community factor was very strong and people rushed to help anyone in need, without waiting to be called to do so. Today, most of us are too busy to visit people or care for them. And the little time we have is spent before the idiot box.

All these factors have brought in a kind of isolation and loneliness in people. Loneliness brings with it depression and pessimism as well as cynicism. These are the fallouts that appear in the lonely lives. This is especially true for people who live in metropolitan cities where the apartments are big barriers to community living.

One has to just enter one of the old-age homes to realise the depth of loneliness suffered by the neglected and old. The misery of isolation is written large on their hapless faces.

Human beings cannot live in isolation. We need others around us. It is said that the worst kind of torture is that of loneliness. It can drive people crazy. Developing stable relationships guarantees emotional security and success.

Negative thoughts are more likely to crop up when a person is lonely. Self-doubt, lack of confidence, fears, phobias and what not can occur only when there is void around you. When you are surrounded by loving friends or family, these ghosts of negativity will keep far away from you.

Says Norman Vincent Peale, 'In the first place, start to like other people. How do you do this? One of the most successful ways is through positive thinking. Positive thinkers become out-flowing personalities, they cease to be obsessively concerned about themselves, and they begin to be concerned for others. They "love everybody", and once they begin to do so, they themselves become lovable. They are sought out, needed personalities.'

Loneliness follows solitude, isolation, abandonment, or even the sense that others do not care, do not understand or cannot offer their support. Loneliness is greatest in countries that value independence as opposed to those societies in which community living and working together is the norm.

Loneliness causes a level of emotional pain that makes it difficult to make friends and meet new people. The greater the loneliness, the harder it is to remedy, a bitter catch-22. Therefore, the first logical step in alleviating loneliness is addressing the emotional pain itself, finding a way to be alone, yet at peace.

There is no investment that is as fruitful as an investment in relationships. Investing in relationship requires time to be spent with people, in a meaningful manner. It means being available for the friends or relatives when they need you and to be emotionally honest with them. If loneliness has taught me anything, it's the value of a friend. Even in a relationship, one can feel lonely. This happens when one becomes habituated and desensitised to the presence of the other person, when one takes the other for granted.

There is a wise old saying that relationships are like sands held in your hand. Held loosely, with an open hand, the sand remains where it is. The minute you close your hand and squeeze tightly, the sand trickles through your fingers. Relationships are like that. Held loosely, with respect and freedom for the other person, a relationship is likely to remain intact. But hold too tightly, too possessively, and the relationship slips away and is lost.

Most of the relationships these days are based on greed and self-interest. The moment you are introduced to someone, the person is likely to begin calculating how much of an asset you will prove to be and whether it is worth investing time on you, and whether you will be able to return the favours granted to you. It is these calculations that come in the way of emotional honesty.

Emotional honesty means to be a part of a relationship without any expectations, just because you like the person or because you enjoy being with him. No ulterior motives or expectations should cloud the relationship. A person who invests in others holistically can never suffer loneliness.

Loneliness is hard to heal. It requires more than just casual social contact. I think some people need to form genuine connections with others on a personal one-to-one basis. Of course, loneliness has led many people to develop friends on the Internet and chat for hours with strangers. Talking with strangers is interesting but not very emotionally meaningful. I think that if loneliness is to heal, it requires more investment of time. It requires an investment in other people and patience and endurance until that investment returns a real, sincere relationship.

Just as a good relationship can be a boon, the reverse is true about a bad one. Nothing is more harmful than living in a toxic relationship. It saps energy, promotes mental trauma and unhappiness. Eventually, such a relationship leads to physical ailments and mental depression. Relationships have their own little subtle games being played between two people, with one grabbing all the power and throwing the other into the shadows.

A toxic relationship is one in which you are feeling harmed either emotionally or physically. It is a relationship in which you are chronically tired, angry or frightened. In a toxic relationship you worry about a safe time to talk to your partner and you do not have the 'right' to express yourself. In short, a relationship that is abusive in any way may be a toxic relationship. It makes us feel small or worthless. One of the most important things to remember about being in a toxic relationship is that you do have choices and you can get out of it.

How do you know if you are in a toxic relationship?

If the reply to more than two is a 'yes', you are trapped in a destructive relationship.

There is a nagging feeling of insecurity.

You are made to feel inferior.

Every conversation leads to argument of some sort.

You are not secure enough to share your secrets or failures with the person.

You are on the defensive most of the time.

You are always on the alert to spot the hidden meaning in each statement.

Why don't people opt out of such relationships that are damaging to their mind and body?

Unfortunately, a lot of us cling to relationships which are dysfunctional, because we feel we have nowhere else to go. We stick on to the unfaithful boyfriend or the deceiving friend only because we feel lost and lonely without them. A lot of people accept all the physical and mental abuse due to low self-worth. Lack of confidence or low self-esteem can be a reason why people remain in a toxic relationship. Or it can be depression, fear of being alone, or threats from the hurtful partner. However, it is best to opt out of a relationship that is robbing you of peace and happiness. The fear of consequences hamper the severing of the relationship in most cases, but the awareness that life can be more meaningful once a person has moved on can bridge that fear.

Detoxifying relationships

Among healers the sharing of energy is referred to as cording. This cord represents emotions and feelings connecting two individuals together. Babies are born with the umbilical cord attaching them to their mothers. But there comes a time for a mother to cut the apron strings, allowing her child to go out into the world on its own. If the mother fails to break the cord, the child will eventually attempt to do it.

The world is full of unhealthy relationships. In these relationships, individuals cling to one another allowing cord attachments to occur between them. Seldom is the sharing done equally. Actually if the energy sharing was done equally, it would be silly to have the cord in place at all. It is possible to be in a relationship without cording one another; in fact, it is preferable. Couples that share one life source ordinarily create a relationship in which one individual becomes weaker, the other stronger. The weakened person feels helpless because s/he is receiving less space and energy. The stronger person feels great for a time, but his/her appetite may increase, craving more of the shared space and energy.

There are many difficult situations that we face in life. Making those situations work for us as a couple requires serious effort. Many find it easier to end the relationship than work on it. It doesn't matter if you were the person who walked away or if someone else left you; a loss is felt either way. It is especially painful if a relationship ends without closure. Unfortunately, sometimes when people 'break up', what they don't realise is that they may still have their cords attached. The intact cord keeps an open channel for continuous feeding on each other's emotions and anxieties.

If you experience pain from an estranged relationship or troubled marriage, you could try either the bridge visualisation or infinity exercise to gently release the cord attachment and free yourself of continued feelings of sadness or separation.

Bridge visualisation

To do this exercise visualise a walking bridge in your mind. Imagine yourself standing on the far end of this bridge. Now imagine the person you want to cut cords with is standing on the opposite end of the bridge. When you feel ready to energetically connect with the other person, begin walking slowly to the middle of the bridge. Allow the other person to walk towards you, meeting you half way.

Once you are in eye contact with one another, you may begin communicating with an inner dialogue. Tell the person what your feelings are. This is not a time to be angry or to hold onto grudges – you are releasing the ties. Tell the person that you are sorry for all of the things you said or did that hurt him/her. Tell him/her that you are forgiving him/her for all the hurtful things that were said or done in your relationship. Say your good-byes, wishing each other well in your separateness. Turn around and walk off the bridge.

Note: It is okay if the other person remains on the bridge as they may not be as ready to be disconnected from you as you are and it may take some adjusting on his/her part to get used to being outside of your energy.

Infinity exercise

This exercise is done with another person. If the person you wish to break the emotional cords with is willing to participate, this is extremely helpful. Otherwise choose someone who is willing to act as a surrogate of the person you wish to cut bonds with.

Two persons face each other while standing 6–8 feet apart from one another. Visualise the infinity sign (number 8 sideways) being traced again and again in a continuous cycle. Each crossing of the infinity sign between you symbolises severing the cord that is keeping you emotionally attached.

This exercise can be done silently or with conversations of forgiveness and closure. You may like to visualise the encircling tracings in different colours as you deal with different feelings during this session. For instance, you could visualise the colour red for releasing passions or feelings of anger, pink or green for calming heartaches, and so on. Repeat this exercise until you feel satisfied that separation has occurred.

Two therapies that are creating ripples in the recent years are:

1. Holotropic Breathwork
2. Rebirthing.

Reputed to be very effective in dealing with repressed emotions and emotional cleansing, these therapies are the hot news in the psychotherapy world.

1. Holotropic Breathwork

Holotropic Breathwork was developed by Stanislov and Christina Grof during the 1970s and 1980s. In 1974, after 10 years of yoga practice, Christina Grof had a sudden experience of life-force energy and change in consciousness during a meditation period led by a Siddha yoga master. This led to a roller coaster of emotional experiences over the next year. In

1975, Christina Grof was referred to Dr Stan Grof, who helped her by staying with the emotions and moving through them. In the late 1970s, Stan and Christina Grof got together in California and began to develop Holotropic Breathwork.

The Procedure: Holotropic Breathwork is usually conducted in a workshop or class setting, under the guidance of a facilitator. It begins with each individual in the group discussing the key issues in their life. The group is then divided into partners. Each person in the pair takes turns as a breather and a sitter. The sitter provides emotional support, reminders to breathe, and material things like cushions or blankets to keep the breather comfortable.

The breather lies down on a mat and uses blankets, if necessary, for extra warmth. The breathwork facilitator then leads a brief relaxation exercise.

With soft music in the background, the breather begins breathing faster and deeper as instructed by the facilitator. The breathing process is up to the breather. Some people ask their sitters to remind them to breath faster and deeper (often by a light touch of the shoulder) if they begin to fall asleep early on in the process. If pain or tension appears in the body during the process and is not resolved by the breath, the facilitator offers focused bodywork.

During the breathwork process, the breather can have quite a wide range of possible experiences. Such experiences can include deep feelings of joy or serenity, yogic sleep/meditative states, re-experience of traumas or the birth process, bodily sensations (tension, pain, warmth, etc.), crying, yelling, body movements, transpersonal experiences such as past life experiences, etc.

It is important to try and avoid directing the process to go to a particular place. Whatever happens is okay. With the help of the breath, evocative music, a safe atmosphere, relaxation, and a willingness to embrace the experiences, the unconscious part of the mind will take you to wherever you need to go for inner healing and transformation.

2. Rebirthing

Rebirthing is a healing process that engages with the mind, the body and the spirit to cleanse away toxic patterns of being and facilitate new, healthy and fulfilling goals and choices. The core practice of Rebirthing is a breathing technique; the core metaphor is the rebirth of the personality through the integration of suppressed experience.

It is a simple breathing rhythm that helps connect to deep unconscious levels. Past memories may be experienced and emotional blockages cleared. It can be a powerful technique for restoring a physical, emotional and spiritual balance. It is a journey into an unfolding of our soul's potential. It takes us to an awareness of our passions, desires, choices and goals in life – the soul's purpose, which is often obscured behind negativity and self-doubt.

Rebirthing uses a combination of skilled counselling and body-orientated therapy involving a particular mode of circular breathing. It is simple and powerful, yet a gentle healing process that dissolves tension and stress in the body, while integrating the body and mind into a new liveliness and wholeness.

Accepting responsibility

Paradoxically, by trying to avoid pain by suppression we suppress those parts of ourselves that we have learned to disapprove of, or to judge negatively. We split off painful feelings: guilt, shame, longing and neediness. But the knowledge that somewhere deep down they are still there haunts us and makes us fearful of exploring our psyches.

Rebirthing allows the body to remember and integrate 'disowned' states; it purifies and cleanses the chakra system of the body; it relaxes and nourishes; and most importantly, it can lead one into a new spiritual reality – a place of deeper trust and security.

On a wider level it may enhance an understanding of our place in this present quantum leap in consciousness on our planet. It is true that as we heal our 'victim consciousness', we empower ourselves to become a more open and clear channel for the creation of a new world from the truth within.

The Procedure: It requires a person to lie on the back with her body relaxed and hands by the sides, in an open posture. The diaphragm, the chest, all of the person's breathing apparatuses are utilised. The breath is termed connected because there is no pause at the end of either the inhalation or exhalation. The exhalation is open, relaxed and effortless. The inhalation may be fast or deep, or both, depending on the stage in the process. At the start of the session the focus is on a strong inhalation to the top of the chest up to the fifth chakra, the throat, the seat of expression. The breath can activate all the chakras, but without enabling expression the energy will be blocked. All this stimulates feeling and experience in the body and various sensations can rapidly arise – for example, tingling in the limbs, or cramp in the hands or around the mouth.

Rather than trying to alleviate the sensations through twitching or stretching, the person is encouraged to relax into them and to experience the feelings that may lie beneath. The Rebirthing breath is not hyperventilation, and the sensations of panic associated with hyperventilation do not appear. It is a cure for the sub-ventilation that most of us make do with for most of our day. Just think of the occasions when we do breathe fully, during some peak experience – competitive sport, mountain climbing, lovemaking – to recall how exhilarated and connected, how whole the mind, body and spirit can be.

What occurs during Rebirthing differs from person to person and session to session: Sometimes the experience is euphoric, at other times scary or sad, bringing up material that may be very uncomfortable. The Rebirther is there to support the person in exploring areas they might normally avoid, and to continue to guide the breathing. At the end of the process the person can turn on to the side in a foetal position, breathe gently and integrate the experiences of the session.

The process of rebirthing brings the suppressed emotions to the surface, from the unconscious, reducing its power to sabotage our lives and giving us the opportunity to forgive and let go of hurt from the past.

RECAP

- Certain relationships can be toxic in nature.
- A relationship that is abusive in any way may be a toxic relationship.
- A toxic relationship is one in which you are feeling harmed either emotionally or physically.
- It is a relationship in which you are chronically tired, angry or frightened.

▶▶

- A relationship that is abusive in any way may be a toxic relationship.
- Sometimes we tend to hold on to certain emotions after severing a relationship. These continue to haunt our minds and cause sickness. There are therapies like bridging and infinity exercises to get rid of the residual emotions.
- Therapies like Rebirthing and Breathwork also help in clearing the emotional blocks.

25

TOXIC ANGER

Anger is one of the most toxic emotions and gives birth to a host of diseases. It is violent, invasive and exhausting. It raises blood pressure, disturbs mental equilibrium and plays havoc with general health. An angry person cannot make rational decisions. Choleric people are prone to ulcers, hypertension, backache, migraine and heart problems. Suppressing anger is detrimental to overall well-being, which can lead to bowel problems, respiratory ills and skin flare-ups. Expressing anger and ventilating angry feelings is the first step towards control of that emotion. Women are much more likely than men to turn anger inwards and blame themselves, thus becoming depressed. There are many ways by which one can get rid of anger without hurting anyone.

Repressed anger can result in resentment, anxiety or depression, all of which are damaging to the health. It is like a time bomb ticking away in your brain, likely to explode at any moment.

A recent study conducted by researchers at Yale University School of Medicine in Connecticut suggests that heightened emotion such as anger might lead to premature cardiac contractions.

There would hardly be a person on this earth who has never felt anger at some point of his life. The extent may vary, but we have all experienced anger and its repercussions. Anger is a normal and even necessary emotion. But when anger is uncontrolled, it can cause problems in your job, your personal relationships and health. Uncontrolled anger is toxic in nature.

Anger is described as a strong feeling of displeasure. There are many things that may cause you to become angry, it could be an action of another person, an event, or worrying about personal problems in your life can also cause anger. Sometimes it so happens that you remember an event that initially caused you to get angry, and get angry all over again. In this case it is memories which cause renewed anger.

If you are angry and opt to express it, be responsible for the consequences of such an act. Not only would you raise your blood pressure, but you would harm your relationships with others. On the other hand, not expressing it would keep the anger simmering within you, which could be more harmful.

How do you express your anger?

The commonest way to express anger is through aggression. Aggression is the instinctive, natural way to express anger. In certain situations, the aggression that comes from being angry may actually serve to protect you. Anger is an intuitive response to a threat. For this reason, a certain amount of anger is beneficial. On the other hand, anger should not be allowed to turn into rage that causes one to lash out physically at other people or objects. If you punch a wall or hit someone when you are angry, your anger is probably uncontrollable and could be dangerous to you as well as others.

Expressed anger is not necessarily worse than suppressed anger. Suppressed anger can cause hypertension, high blood pressure and even depression. It may cause you to display passive aggressive behaviours, or to be constantly grumpy, moody or cynical.

Why do people get aggressive?

According to psychologists, aggression is angry, hostile behaviour that is intended to upset or hurt others. Research also shows that the male of the species are more aggressive in behaviour than the females.

Aggression can take either physical form or verbal. Physical aggression isn't as common as the verbal ones, especially in adults. Verbal aggression may employ the use of abusive language.

Getting your anger out is supposed to be cathartic and can help dissipate hostility. But behaviour specialists have found that venting anger on inanimate objects by acts like punching a pillow or hitting a punching bag increases rather than decreases aggressive behaviour.

Are you constantly grumpy, moody or cynical? These symptoms are displayed by constantly putting others down, criticising or insulting everything and everybody and repeatedly making cynical or sarcastic comments.

Do you get too angry?

Doctors, counsellors or psychiatrists can give you a test that can measure your angry feelings to determine how well you handle your anger. If you answer 'yes' to any of these questions, you may have a problem with your anger:

Does your anger turn into violence, causing you to hit, kick, punch, push or physically damage another person or object?

Has anyone told you that you need to control your temper?

Have you had problems with the law as a result of your temper?

26

ANGER MANAGEMENT

Tips on anger management

You can't get rid of all of the anger in your life. Since anger is a normal feeling, there will always be circumstances that cause you to get angry. Learning to control your anger is the key.

Express your anger in a healthy way. Don't hit, kick or push anyone or anything. If you have physical anger that must be expelled, take up a sport such as karate or kickboxing to help release your frustrations. You could also invest in a punching bag and hit it whenever you are feeling angry.

Express your needs. We often get angry when our needs aren't met. Make it a habit to discuss your needs before you explode in rage. Perhaps the other person doesn't realise that you are feeling unsatisfied.

Try relaxing. Relaxation methods such as deep breathing may help to calm you down. When you feel yourself getting angry, stop, remove yourself from the situation and take slow deep breaths until you feel a calm returning.

Try yoga or meditation to help you get in touch with your feelings and release pent-up feelings.

Avoid situations that increase frustration and make you feel uncomfortable.

Also steer clear of circumstances that reduce self-esteem. Another thing that one would do well to avoid is comparisons that undermine your capabilities.

Think before you act. Angry people tend to react quickly to a situation, which usually leads to an over-reaction. If you are in a heated discussion or you feel yourself getting angry, stop. Don't say the first thing that comes to mind, think carefully about what you want to say. How many times have you reacted in anger and later thought, 'I shouldn't have said that'? Think first, and then speak.

Change the way you think. This may be easier said than done, and it will take some practice. The next time you feel yourself getting angry, instead of cursing and swearing, tell yourself, 'I'm mad, but I can deal with this.' Control the anger instead of letting it control you.

Do you need counselling for your anger? If you feel that you are not able to control your anger or if your temper is causing problems at work or in your personal relationships, counselling may help you learn to control your anger.

RECAP

- Anger is one of the most toxic emotions and gives birth to a host of diseases.
- It raises blood pressure, disturbs mental equilibrium and plays havoc with general health.
- It can lead to bowel problems, respiratory ills and skin flare-ups.

▶▶

- ➥ Repressed anger can result in resentment, anxiety or depression, all of which are damaging to the health.
- ➥ Anger management is the art of expressing the emotion without hurting anyone.

27

ALTERING THE ATTITUDE

In the course of life, most people exhibit a certain way of thinking and reacting to most situations, and the outcome of all their reactions determines the success rate of their efforts. While a lot of people are socially most acceptable because of their positive attitude towards everything they come across, there are several who lose a winning game only because of their negative attitude.

By thinking positive, many hurdles can be crossed and lot more can be achieved even when the going is tough. Positive thoughts can give a mental strength to deal with most adverse situations in life. On the other hand, negative factors play a very destructive role in the build-up of a person's psyche. They colour judgements, thoughts and reactions to a large extent.

Negative emotions can also be the harbingers of various ailments that manifest in physical form. Although this fact has long been recognised by all the physicians, not much importance was given to this aspect till recently. The expression 'A healthy mind in a healthy body' has been around for ages, but now a little modification to that statement would be in order. A more apt expression would read: 'Healthy emotions keep the body healthy.'

A person with a positive attitude is highly motivated, self-confident with high level of self-worth, and is essentially a good communicator. But a person with a negative attitude displays a low self-esteem, lack of motivation and visible signs of depression at failing, and generally has poor communication ability.

Negative emotions like anger, jealousy and frustration lead to mental stress, and this in turn leads to several ailments like high blood pressure, ulcers, etc. Chronic anger, discontent and hatred activate powerful brain chemicals that literally poison our whole system and weaken our immunity. Similarly, chronic anxiety and toxic anger have already been established as cancer risks. This has to do with stress hormones and their suppressing effect on the immune system, as well as on many other vital, physiological functions. Anger has been known to be particularly hard on the liver. So have jealousy and envy.

Chronic depression has been proven to slow the whole physiology. Apart from hampering digestion, it has a dulling effect on one's mind, and affects the spontaneity of reactions adversely. This could be very dangerous for a person who works in a factory assembly line or drives a vehicle.

It was Herbert Benson who discovered the link between the state of mind and physical health. A National Institute Health panel in the USA recently decreed that relaxation therapies are effective in treating chronic pain. Privately repeating words or sounds while ignoring intruding thoughts, can significantly ease the pain in lower back problems, arthritis and headaches. Pleasant and positive thoughts could bring a soothing effect, while the negative ones could disturb and cause turbulence of the mental kind. Benson's early research, as far as 25 years back, had shown the fact that meditation could lower blood pressure.

It is not only the negative emotions that play havoc with a person's personality, but the attitude born out of a mix of negative factors can create behavioural problems in most people. It is surprising how many people would rather deal with a pleasant and positive person and avoid a person with a negative attitude even when he is talented. The negative attitude makes a person rigid and uncompromising. Negativity also breeds cynicism.

It is said that people who display a negative attitude generally have gone through a lot of adversity and that has built up the wall of cynicism around them, which in turn colours their attitude. Often it is these people who react with statements like 'It is not possible', 'I don't think it can be done', and 'I won't be able to do it', etc., whereas a person with a positive thinking will react with typical sentences like 'Well, let's try it out', 'It may certainly be possible' or 'No harm in trying'.

It is this difference in attitudes that could decide between success and failure. Everything in life revolves around the decisions one makes, whether it is the relationships, career or any other aspect of living. Children who are brought up in a loving atmosphere where they are accepted as they are, unconditionally, grow up to be mature adults who do not find it difficult to adjust to demanding situations. They are easy-going and friendly by nature.

Abhishek has gone through a life that reads like fiction. Having lost his parents in a road accident, he suffered the rebukes and taunts of his aunt who had brought him up with an iron hand. His negative attitude stemmed from the negative forces that surrounded his life. This cost him his girlfriend's love, several friendships and finally his job. Abhishek woke up to the fact one day while he was attending a spiritual discourse to which a friend had dragged him. Initially sceptic, he was surprised to find the influence the discourse ultimately had on him. That proved to be the turning point in his life. Abhishek decided to give a new twist to his life by wilfully changing his outlook and thinking.

It was no mean task. One factor that helped him carry out his resolution was his utter belief in the Supreme Being. Hours of meditation and spiritual discourses helped cleanse his mental framework giving it a fresh lease of thought, replacing the negative ones with the positive. The hard work ultimately paid off. Today, he is a successful man, a happy husband and a doting parent.

'I make a determined effort to reinforce positive thoughts in my children. Parents are responsible for the attitude of their children to a large extent, and it is our duty to impart the right directional forces in our children so that they can develop a positive and healthy attitude,' he says.

According to Satya Grover, a psychotherapist, 'The complex pattern of reactions is scripted very early in life. Within the first five years of life, most of this script is written, and thereafter it is the replay which keeps occurring for various situations and circumstances. Therefore, it becomes very important for the parents to nurture their child with the right attitude.'

Self-esteem of a person is totally dependent on his attitude in life. Those who have suffered rejection, rebukes and conditional love are the victims of a low self-esteem, whereas children who have received unconditional love and acceptance from their parents are bound to be more confident and self-assured. While factors like peer groups, school environment, social environment and friends do influence the building up of a child's psyche, it is the home environment which largely moulds the personality. Parents, teachers and friends are the main influence that determines the attitude one would carry throughout his life.

All religions profess the value of positive thinking, and a truly religious person does not find it difficult to practise a positive attitude. Methods like meditation, Reiki, Vipassana, etc. help in the cleansing of the mind. They advocate the purification of mind and developing control over the baser instincts and thoughts, finally replacing them with the positive thoughts. The mind control helps in channelising the energies into positive paths, which in turn create a healthy aura in the environment.

Some time back, an eminent psychologist had designed a method for the outlet and identification of negative feelings. He advised those filled with doubts and fears to fill out two sheets of paper, giving one the heading negative, the other, positive. The negative thoughts and feelings were put down on the sheet, which was then torn and burnt. This was a symbol of his intention of discarding the negative behaviour. His method recommended that a person read the positive points on the other sheet, every night, before going to bed. This helped in the induction of positive currents into the person.

The power of positive thinking is so tremendous that it can elevate one's energy level to an astounding level and bring about feats that seem impossible. It is foolhardy to believe that one can remain at a peak level of positive thinking every hour or every day. The curve for positive thinking can be compared to the curve one tries to establish for prosperity and success. No rational businessman believes that the curve of prosperity will keep on mounting every month, with never a single dip. After one reaches the sharp peak, there is always a ride that goes a little below the peak. Positive thoughts produce energy that invigorates and causes an upliftment of the spirit in the truest sense. Auto-suggestion of a positive nature helps in overriding the negative thoughts. Taking a positive attitude can be a turning points in one's life especially when things are not really working out in one's favour. It is the defeatist attitude and negative thinking which will get you down and keep you down during times of adversity.

Avoiding negative thoughts does not mean being afraid of them. One should learn to turn them to positive uses. If one is ashamed of the negative thoughts, suppressing them could lead to dangerous result. What is required is an emotional balance where one can acknowledge the emotional reactions and express them without causing any damage to anyone. Repressed negative thoughts could lead to anxiety, depression and contribute to illness such as migraine, blood pressure or backache.

When you hate but dare not admit it even to yourself, the bottled-up hate may make you physically ill. We are all subject to certain emotions that are usually labelled negative but these emotions can be controlled. They do not have to be bottled up inside but can be converted into positive emotions. Energy that is born out of negative thoughts and directed in destructive fields leads to quick burnout, whereas positive energy is exhilarating and unending.

Two friends were walking in the park. Just as they turned the corner, dark and threatening clouds covered the skies, and soon a torrent of heavy showers compelled them to take cover under a tree. One of them remarked, 'There goes our walk. Why did it have to start raining just now?'

The other said, 'It is so beautiful. I could stand here the entire day, watching the rain fall on the parched earth, giving it a new lease of life. Look at the leaves and flowers, they almost seem to be singing with joy at the advent of the monsoon showers after a long dry spell.'

The chasm of opinion between the two friends was as wide as that between the negative and the positive points of view. While one rejoiced in the rain, the other went into a grumbling mode. Basically, it is a matter of attitude. Almost every event can be viewed in two different ways – negative or positive.

While the positive attitude helps us surface over the events with pleasure, in anticipation of something good waiting for us around the corner, the negative attitude can turn us into cynical and pessimistic individuals who find everything wrong in every event.

We are bombarded by negative messages through television, radio, newsprint, and now via the Internet as well. Death, destruction, tragic events surround us from all sides. There is war, disease, shortages, droughts, loss of life and limb, in fact everything bad that one can imagine, happening all around.

There is a difference between blindly ignoring the reality of the world and seeing reality and still looking for the positives. The world can be a cruel place. There is crime, unhappiness and disease. The world can also be a wonderful place. There is love, compassion and joy. Both scenarios exist and will affect us in our lives. Attitude is a major factor. It is the crucial difference between optimism and pessimism. It is the difference that exists between the two opinions – the glass half-full or half-empty. For an optimistic person, there are no barriers – everything swings on well-oiled hinges.

Fyodor Mikhailovich Dostoevsky, the famous Russian novelist who lived between 1821 and 1881, led a life that was full of significance, but it was also fraught with danger. His books like *Crime and Punishment, The Idiot, The Brothers Karamazov* are nothing less than classics.

Dostoevsky spent a significant part of his youth in the army before he took up writing. At one stage of his life, he got involved in a plot against the government. Unfortunately, he was caught, and a court sentenced him to death. As luck would have it, his death sentence was commuted to a spell of imprisonment in Siberia. Eventually he was released, and when he got back to European Russia, he started up a magazine called *The Times.*

His magazine was very critical of the government, and Dostoevsky was forced to close it down. Several times he tried to re-establish the magazine but didn't succeed in doing so. Instead he got into debt and had to leave the country. If anything, he was a born optimist who found something positive in every situation.

Neither his death sentence nor its commutation to imprisonment in Siberia, nor the forced closure of his magazine, could rob him of his positive mindset, and he continued to pen his novels, which ultimately made him a famous name in the world.

Is it easy to maintain a positive attitude at all times? No, it isn't, and let no one tell you otherwise. Despite our best resolutions, we are likely to falter in the path of being positive. Philosophers tell us that we should treat the reverses in our life as learning experiences. But what happens when a 'learning experience' hits us hard and ruins our lives? How many of us are able to persevere and continue on the enlightened spiritual path. Most of us want to lead our lives according to the situational demands. Hardships become a learning experience only when we view them in an objective light and can remain detached to the results that follow the hardships.

RECAP

- Positive thoughts can give a mental strength to deal with most adverse situations in life.
- Auto-suggestion of a positive nature helps in overriding the negative thoughts.

▶▶

- ➥ Energy that is born out of negative thoughts leads to a quick burnout, whereas positive energy is exhilarating.
- ➥ Emotional control is achieved by learning to put the negative thoughts to positive use.

SECTION V

28

EMOTIONAL DETOXIFICATION

Emotional toxins are like roadblocks on the highway to Happiness Ville. Just as you are driving at top gear to your destination, you hit this roadblock. There is no escape – you can't move it, and you can't move over it; the only way out is to steer around it. That is the way you have to go around the emotional roadblocks in your life. If you find them too heavy to be moved and taken out of your path, steer around them!

Toxic emotions brutalise and scar the soul, upset the mind and cause physical ailments. Emotional toxicity can be as lethal as the physical one. It can bring about ailments that can be cured by no other medicine than emotional detoxification. Since the physical, mental and emotional aspects are interrelated, the healing of one depends on each of the other elements. This fact is recognised by scientists and doctors today. Within our universe are both positive and negative energies. Positive energy is: light, goodness, kindness, love, patience, charity, hope, etc. Negative is: darkness, hatred, fear, unkindness, intolerance, selfishness, despair, discouragement, etc.

Hatred, anger and jealousy are as intricately woven into our psyche as love, affection, compassion and concern. Fear is an emotion that is a huge hurdle to living a more relaxed life. Fear is an emotion conjured up within us in response to perceived danger. Sometimes that danger is real, but often it is imagined.

Whether you fear public speaking or 'the future', heights or spiders, fear is extremely stressful. One of the best ways to control irrational fear is through a slow process of desensitisation. Build up your tolerance one step at a time. If you are terrified of heights, force yourself to stand a little above the ground and look down. Repeat affirmation like 'I have risen above the fear of heights'. Gradually, work your way to greater heights using the same affirmation.

According to Mark Twain, 'Do the thing you fear the most, and the death of fear is certain.'

Accepting emotions

When we repress our feelings, they come out in other self-destructive ways. While some people resort to venting the repressed emotions by overeating or by becoming anorexic, others fall victim to drugs, alcohol, smoking or depression. No one can remain positive all the time. You are bound to have your share of negative as well as positive emotions. It is normal to feel bad and express it. You will be emotionally healthier if you accept rather than deny the negatives.

All of us must have suffered from the feelings of resentment at some time or the other. When we were children, we might have resented a classmate who seemed to have the things we didn't have. As teenagers we might have resented the boy who got the girl we adored, and then as adults we might have resented colleagues who bypassed us in career. It is a part of life. Imagine what would happen if we tried to suppress our resentment. Resentment robs us of vital emotional energy, but suppressed resentment makes us bankrupt.

Whenever you find yourself resenting someone, try to figure out why you resent him or her. Being objective about the point of resentment sometimes brings about a transformation. Do you realise that the person you resent may have his own grievances against you? The most awful fact about a negative emotion is that it generates more negativity around you. As you spread the negative energies and throw them into the atmosphere, they return manifold to you. For instance, if you sow the seeds of hatred, you will certainly reap a bumper crop of hatred. Now it is up to you to use that crop or destroy it. On the contrary, if you spread the positive energy of love around you, you will receive it back with dividend from all sides.

Each person has the choice. He can fill his soul with love and positive energy or dissipate itself with negative vibes and destructive energy. Love doesn't need verbal expressions all the time. It can be expressed in various acts like a smile, a word of encouragement and a small act of sacrifice. If all this is not possible, the simple acts of transforming the negative thoughts or acts can work wonders in clearing the emotional blocks. By controlling anger, hate, envy, bitterness and being forgiving we can transcend to greater heights. The negative emotions destroy the soul while the positive ones elevate it to the spiritual realm.

Positive and negative energies work in opposition to each other. When we internalise these energies, they become our servants. Positive attracts the positive, and negative attracts negative. By the simple act of thinking positive thoughts and speaking positive words we attract positive energy.

If we were to opt for a world full of negative feelings and vibes, it is doubtful if anyone would opt for such a world. We expect things to work positively around us, then why should we contribute negativity to the atmosphere around us? Happiness, healing, peace and joy can only happen when we have managed to clear our emotional blocks and replaced the negative energies with the positive ones.

There is tremendous power in our thoughts. It is the soul that has the power to control the mind and mind controls the body. So you see, how important it is for us to strengthen the soul. All our physical, mental and spiritual healing takes place when we release positive energies around us.

There is no experience that is totally negative. There is always something positive in every event, and it is for us to recognise that. Even failures are nothing but learning experiences. None of us is perfect, we are here to make mistakes and learn from these mistakes.

RECAP

- Emotional toxins are like roadblocks on the highway to Happiness Ville.
- Toxic emotions are very harmful. They brutalise and scar the soul, upset the mind and cause physical ailments.
- Since the physical, mental and emotional aspects are interrelated, the healing of one depends on each of the other elements.
- The first step to healing emotional toxicity is the acceptance of negative emotions.
- Repression of emotions manifests in other self-destructive ways.

➥ Each person has the choice. He can fill his soul with love and positive energy or dissipate it with negative vibes and destructive energy.

29

THE EMOTIONAL BAGGAGE

Excess emotional baggage can be genetic or environmental, or a combination of both the factors. Some of the most devastating emotional problems come in packages like disappointing children, a really dead-end job, a highly incompatible marriage, intolerable relatives, an out-of-control debt, a cheating spouse or a really silly dalliance that takes the wind out of your sails. They sap your energy and make life unbearable. Severe emotional trauma can be caused by violent and toxic relationships. They can throw life out of gear and reduce one to an emotional wreck.

'Emotional baggage' is a phrase that has come into vogue in the past couple of decades. Even though the phrase is relatively new, what it describes is as old as mankind. 'Emotional baggage' refers to the residual effects of painful life experiences that we fail to resolve, and which therefore victimise us throughout our lives.

Whether we realise it or not, all of us without exception carry a lot of 'emotional baggage' throughout our lives. For some of us, the suitcase of 'emotional baggage' is a little fuller than that of others. For many of us this baggage can be enough to fill a knapsack, a suitcase or a huge truck.

Emotional baggage is connected to four elements:

Level of self-respect
Self image
Belief system
The ability to deal with the emotional pain

First, identify the problem. Write it down on a piece of paper, so that you can look at it clearly and logically. What really happened? Why did it hurt you? Has this problem occurred in past relationships? How long has this problem been going on?

Second, if you sit and blame some other person for doing all the wrong things to you, you will feel like a victim. You will learn nothing and be doomed to repeat it indefinitely. Rather, accept responsibility for what happened. Say, 'I allowed you to do this to me, and I won't allow you to do that anymore.'

Will these changes happen overnight? No. There are no quick fixes for people who have been emotionally abused. You'll be tested in every new relationship you enter and probably have to walk away from several relationships you're in now. But it's well worth it.

To get rid of the additional burden, we need to accept the fact every one of us has 'emotional baggage'. Once we have admitted to ourselves that we are carrying excess 'emotional baggage,' we need to accept the fact that our 'emotional baggage' is weighing us down. When you travel by airlines, you have to pay for the excess baggage. Similarly, you have to pay in life for carrying emotional baggage too. The best recourse would be to shed all the extra stuff that weighs heavy on the soul. Whether we like to hear it or not, there are opinions to which we hold, acts which we perform and ways in which we relate to one another which are the results of our 'emotional baggage'.

Lastly, having accepted the presence of our emotional baggage, we need to confront and resolve the issue, so that it will no longer have the upper hand to influence what we believe, what we do and how we relate to one another. Such confrontation and resolution can take place through humble reflection and prayer, honest conversation with people who know and love us, or in the context of professional counselling.

Like a wise person told me, 'Like everyone, I have a lot of emotional baggage. However, to keep it from getting too heavy I fill it with humour and wisdom.'

Put it in writing

One way of getting rid of depression and other negative feelings is to get paper and pen and write everything down. Unhappiness, hatred, envy, despair, jealousy, resentment, vindictiveness – let all the problems that have been building up tumble out of your mind onto the paper!

Don't be afraid to own up these feelings. You are not the only one facing negative feelings. All these are natural feelings that tend to surface during our lives when circumstances trigger them off.

Keep writing your feelings down until you are sick of writing. Whatever you do, don't read through what you have written. Let it go. We are rather like computers, and reading the information would store it again. Tear the paper into small pieces and put them in a container and set fire to the paper, preferably outdoors. Reduce the whole thing to ashes, and start your life afresh.

This is also an excellent way of getting rid of all the things that you'd like to say to other people, but don't dare say or don't want to hurt them with. Vent those thoughts on paper, and finish with it.

You don't need all that rubbish; allowing it to build up inside you will only lead to illnesses of the mind and body. Cleanse yourself of unnecessary burden. We acquire so much of the additional negative baggage that frequent and regular cleansing is an absolute necessity. It will help you to be in control of your life.

RECAP

- All our physical, mental and spiritual healing takes place when we release positive energies around us.
- 'Emotional baggage' refers to the residual effects of painful life experiences that we fail to resolve, and which therefore victimise us throughout our lives.
- We need to confront and resolve the repressed issues so that they will no longer have the upper hand to influence what we believe, what we do and how we relate to one another.

30

THE SEVEN DEADLY SINS

We have all heard of the seven deadly sins which were outlined by Pope Gregory the Great in the sixth century. These sins are as relevant today as they were in the sixth century. They continue to prey on the human mind and cause emotional toxicity. Whether it is lust or anger or envy, the deadly emotions are still around and increasing to alarming proportions.

Pride is also known as Vanity.

Envy is the desire for others' traits, status, abilities or situation.

Gluttony is an inordinate desire to consume more than one requires.

Lust is an inordinate craving for the pleasures of the body.

Anger is manifested in the individual who spurns love and opts instead for fury. It is also known as Wrath.

Greed is the desire for material wealth or gain, ignoring the realm of the spiritual. It is also called Avarice or Covetousness.

Sloth is the avoidance of physical or spiritual work.

Wise men advise against harbouring these emotions and replacing them with the seven virtues.

The seven virtues

Faith: belief, trust, loyalty, fidelity and conviction.
Hope: desire, belief, reliance and expectation.
Charity: generosity, benevolence, helpfulness, mercy.
Fortitude: strength, courage, endurance and resoluteness.
Justice: impartiality, fairness, equity, rightness and dispassion.
Temperance: moderation, restraint, self-control, frugality, sobriety.
Prudence: wisdom, vigilance, carefulness, thoughtfulness and discretion.

Some good, some bad

Negative emotions are energy sapping, whilst the positive ones are energising. A person who can realise this truth can override all the negativity and channel the energy in the right direction.

Anger

Anger is perhaps the most destructive emotion, yet we all feed and harbour it in our hearts without a thought. Right from the tiny baby to the old man, anger is the commonest visible emotion in the world. Have you ever wondered what kind of physiological reactions take place when you are angry? Here are some – noradrenaline and epinephrine, two stress chemicals are released in the body. Over a period of time, these chemicals cause heart problems, heartbeats become faster; arteries dilate to carry the extra blood; muscles tense up; you breathe harder; blood is diverted from other organs to the heart, central nervous system and muscles; glucose level rises; testosterone is increased in men, since all the blood is diverted to other places; digestive system suffers suspension. These are just a few of the physical symptoms; there are deeper and more serious effects on the mind and soul.

Can you imagine the kind of damage these changes can cause? At the same time, repressed anger can cause high blood pressure and depression. It can also lower your immunity towards disease. Suppressed rage can cause blockages in arteries. So what does one do? You have to learn the right technique to diffuse your anger in a non-damaging way. Counting 10, the oldest method to control anger, still works fine. Anger ebbs as time passes, so reacting in a delayed manner will allow you to gain control over yourself. Put your anger in writing – let the paper and pen take the edge out of your emotion. Tear up the paper later as you visualise throwing anger out of your system. But the best method is meditation. It brings calm and peace to the mind and makes a world of difference to your attitude.

When you are angry, don't prolong it, store it or exaggerate it. The sweetest form of anger is when there is no violent outbursts, yelling and screaming, nagging or silent withdrawals. When one is angry, no matter how difficult this may be, it is necessary to resolve the reason and cause of anger.

Hatred

Hatred is a passionate emotion and one that is expressed more often than love. It uses up a lot of energy. How much more productive it could be to use the energy in a constructive manner? When hatred develops, one spends excessive time in conceiving ways of destroying and harming the object of hatred. It also leads to anger and frustration.

If there is something or someone you feel hatred towards, avoid them and ignore them because you can't hate someone who is non-existent. Try this exercise and see how much hatred affects you: Stand in front of a mirror and think about the person you hate. Fill your mind completely with the emotion of hatred and say, 'I hate you' and look at your reflection in the mirror. Repeat the same exercise, but this time think of someone you love and fill your heart with the warmth of love. Now say, 'I love you'. Note the facial expression during the two emotional outbursts. As you express hatred, your face becomes ugly and threatening, but it turns beautiful when you express the emotion of love. I am sure you would love to look beautiful, wouldn't you? Stop making yourself ugly with the ugly emotion of hatred.

Jealousy

Jealousy and insecurity are great pals. They can't exist without each other. An insecure person is jealous, and a jealous person is insecure. Insecurity is an emotion that develops from within. It is the result of a lack of self-confidence, self-worth and self-dignity. It is a feeling that everyone around you is better than you and out to harm you. These feelings give rise to jealousy. An achiever does not achieve because he has trampled all over you. He has achieved because he had toiled hard to succeed. You can do so if you put aside your negative emotions. When you realise this fact, your feelings of insecurity and jealousy will disappear and you will be able to rise above them. Jealousy is a wasteful emotion. It drains your energy just as anger does. You waste time contriving ways to destroy the source of jealousy. Instead, redirect the flow of that energy into doing positive things. Work hard without trying to prove the other worse. No one can take from you what is yours.

Smile and laughter

When you smile, the world smiles with you. Nothing spreads faster than a smile. It brings warmth to the coldest heart and gives security to the most insecure person on earth. It is reassuring and energising, it is a lovely emotion, a true gift of God. Laughter synchronises the listener's brain with that of the speaker so that they are emotionally attuned.

When you smile, the happy hormone endorphin gushes around you, the facial muscles crease, massaging the blood vessels and stimulating the flow of blood. The supply of oxygen and nutrients to the brain are enhanced. De-stressing hormone cortisol is released in the body and you feel good. You spread sunshine and happiness all around you.

When you laugh, the heartbeat quickens and circulation is boosted. The nerves get stimulated and the respiratory system improves. There is more oxygen in the body and the immune system is revved up. Laughter establishes a positive climate and a sense of connection between two people; it brings people together.

A good belly laugh speeds blood up through the body and digestion improves. It relaxes the muscles and perks up the systems but lowers the blood pressure. You feel good and all your pains and aches disappear because a good laugh releases endorphins, which are the nature's painkillers. Laughter reduces blood sugar and increases glucose tolerance in people with diabetes. It is said that a hundred laughs are as good as a 10-minute jog. Recent studies have revealed that laughter helps your blood vessels function better. It is good for your heart and brain, two organs that require the steady flow of oxygen carried in the blood. Dr Michael Miller of the University of Maryland, in a meeting of the American College of Cardiology, reported that in a study of 20 healthy people provoking laughter did as much good for their arteries as aerobic activity. Dr Miller's prescription: '30 minutes of exercise three times a week, and 15 minutes of laughter on a daily basis is probably good for the vascular system.'

Laughter makes you happy, and that happiness spreads to others around you. It makes you beautiful. Need any more reasons to smile?

Generosity

Have you ever experienced the joys of giving? People who live only for themselves are amongst the unhappiest ones I have seen, while those who have little and share those modest possessions are the happiest and most blissful. Sharing brings with it a sense of fulfilment and joy which nothing else can bring. When we live for others or spend some time in caring for others, we do ourselves a lot of good. You may be surprised as to how we can do ourselves any good when we do something for others. That is exactly the point. Whatever good we do for someone usually returns to us in manifold ways. That is the rule of nature. If you give a rupee, it is bound to come back many times over. If you don't believe it, try it out. Besides the monetary return, the good deed does a lot of good to us in many more ways. It brings peace and joy to the heart, and that is the biggest return one can get. There is no wiser investment than love because it is returned with heavy compound interest.

Kindness

I came across these beautiful lines in a poster and would like to share them with you because they can make a great impact on everyone.

'A heart that is blessed with intrinsic kindness is a heart that can withstand any amount of negativity. It can bounce back to healthy and robust positive state no matter what it goes through or no matter what goes through it. Anger, envy, frustration, hatred, anxiety, you name it, and it can digest it and come clean at the end of it all.'

This is all because kindness is capable of wielding great powers, even greater than the seemingly powerful emotions of anger and hatred. The power of kindness comes from its great building strength. It builds bridges of tolerance and understanding between people, between thoughts and between actions. It is at once gentle and strong. In fact, its gentleness is its greatest strength.

So, if you want to be a strong person, go forth and rely on filling your heart with kindness. You may feel uncomfortable for a while, as you and others around you may think that you are a weak person; they might misread the kindness in your heart. But soon everyone, whether he is your deemed friend or foe, will realise your strength through the power of kindness and return to your fold with willingness and reciprocity. When that happens, you know you have conquered the world through kindness. And that is the ultimate power of human heart.

RECAP

➥ Anger is one of the most destructive emotions; hatred is a passionate emotion and one that is expressed more often than love. Both call for the using up of a lot of energy.

➥ Getting your anger out is cathartic and can help dissipate hostility.

▶▶

- Jealousy is a wasteful emotion. It drains your energy just as anger and hatred do.
- A good belly laugh provides as much health benefits as a 10-minute jog.
- Kindness and generosity bring peace and joy to the heart.
- Crying is a natural process of emotional catharsis. It is an ultimate expression of sadness or extreme happiness.

31

THE BODY–EMOTION CONNECTION

In traditional Asian medicine, emotions and physical health are intimately connected. Sadness, nervous tension and anger, worry, fear, and overwork are each associated with a particular organ in the body. For example, irritability and inappropriate anger can affect the liver and result in menstrual pain, headache, redness of the face and eyes, dizziness and dry mouth.

Whereas the western practitioner limits his approach to the physical body, the eastern practitioner will always look at the ailment in a holistic manner. The mental and emotional conditions are always taken into account while making a diagnosis, and the treatment largely depends on the physical as well as emotional state of the patient. The difference does not end here; while the western cures have a single-window approach to a problem, the eastern one has a multiple-window system wherein the same ailment in different individuals is treated differently, based on the individual behaviour. For example, if I were to approach an allopathic practitioner for treatment for an allergic condition, he would prescribe the general medicine given to all patients with allergic conditions, after a diagnostic test is conducted. Almost all patients with the same symptoms would be given the same medicines. If I were to consult an Ayurved or Homeopath, he would dig into things like my preference for hot or cold food, sweet or sour dishes, whether I was hot headed or cool in my behaviour and hundred other things. Only after studying the details would he prescribe a medicine for me, which would be quite different from anything he would give another patient with the same ailment.

The traditional Asian diagnosis is highly individualised. Once the afflicted organ or system is identified, the healer examines the patient's symptoms to determine the treatment and approach.

For instance, if a patient was suffering from breast distension, menstrual pain and irritability during menses and the symptoms point to the liver as the origin for the problems, the healer would use specific herbs and acupuncture points. But if another patient is suffering from migraines, headaches, dizziness and excessive anger, which are again caused by a different kind of liver malfunction, the treatment will differ vastly from the previous one.

What does the liver have to do with migraine headaches? Organ systems in the traditional Asian sense may include the western medical-physiological function, but are also part of a holistic body system. The liver, for example, ensures that energy and blood flow smoothly throughout the body. It also regulates bile secretion, stores blood and is connected with the tendons, nails and eyes. At the same time, the organ is intrinsically connected with emotions of a person. Any imbalance in the emotions can cause a malfunctioning of the specific organ.

By understanding these connections, we can see how an eye disorder such as conjunctivitis might be due to an imbalance in the liver, or excess menstrual flow may be due to dysfunction in the liver's blood-storing ability. Besides emotions, other factors such as dietary, environmental, lifestyle and hereditary factors also contribute to the development of imbalances.

Here are some important organs, their functions and ailments caused due to emotional imbalance:

Spleen

Emotions: Worry, dwelling or focusing too much on a particular topic, excessive mental work.

Spleen Function: Food digestion and nutrient absorption. Helps in the formation of blood and energy. Connected with muscles, mouth and lips. Involved in thinking, studying and memory.

Symptoms of Spleen Imbalance: Tired, loss of appetite, mucus discharge, poor digestion, abdominal distension, loose stools or diarrhoea. Weak muscles, pale lips. Bruising, excess menstrual blood flow and other bleeding disorders.

Lungs

Emotions: Grief, sadness, detachment.

Lung Function: Respiration. Forms energy from air, and helps to distribute it throughout the body. Works with the kidney to regulate water metabolism. Important in the immune system and resistance to viruses and bacteria. Regulates sweat glands and body hair, and provides moisture to the skin.

Symptoms of Lung Imbalance: Shortness of breath and shallow breathing, sweating, fatigue, cough, frequent cold and flu, allergies, asthma and other lung conditions. Dry skin. Depression and crying.

Liver

Emotions: Anger, resentment, frustration, irritability, bitterness.

Liver Function: Involved in the smooth flow of energy and blood throughout the body. Regulates bile secretion, stores blood and is connected with the tendons, nails and eyes.

Symptoms of Liver Imbalance: Breast distension, menstrual pain, headache, irritability, inappropriate anger, dizziness, dry, red eyes and other eye conditions, tendonitis.

Heart

Emotions: Lack of enthusiasm and vitality, mental restlessness, depression, insomnia, despair.

Heart Function: Regulates the heart and blood vessels. Responsible for even and regular pulse. Influences vitality and spirit. Connected with the tongue, complexion and arteries.

Symptoms of Heart Imbalance: Insomnia, heart palpitations and irregular heart beat, excessive dreaming, poor long-term memory, psychological disorders.

Kidney

Emotions: Fearful, weak willpower, insecure, aloof, isolated.

Kidney Function: Key organ for sustaining life. Responsible for reproduction, growth and development, and maturation. Involved with lungs in water metabolism and respiration. Connected with bones, teeth, ears and head hair.

Symptoms of Kidney Imbalance: Frequent urination, urinary incontinence, night sweats, dry mouth, poor short-term memory, low back pain, ringing in the ears, hearing loss, and other ear conditions. Premature grey hair, hair loss and osteoporosis.

RECAP

- Emotions and physical health are intimately connected.
- An eye disorder such as conjunctivitis might be due to an imbalance in the liver, or excess menstrual flow may be due to dysfunction in the liver's blood-storing ability.
- Sadness, nervous tension and anger, worry, fear and overwork are each associated with a particular organ in the body.
- Irritability and inappropriate anger can affect the liver and result in menstrual pain, headache, redness of the face and eyes, dizziness and dry mouth.

32

THE PROCESS OF EMOTIONAL DETOXIFICATION

Although most of us harbour emotional toxins, not many are aware of the harm these toxins can cause. Only when awareness strikes do people make an attempt to cleanse the toxins, and they do so because they want to feel purified. Emotional detoxification brings with it a feeling of lightness, freedom and increased energy. Many of these feel-good factors can be experienced when one undertakes physical detoxification by fasting, juicing and eliminating certain foods, drinks or stimulants, but the experience of holistic detoxification is much more joyful and lasting.

At first, it would seem as though there can be no better experience than the one that occurs after physical detoxification, but as one resorts to it regularly, one begins to realise that there is more to detoxification, than is done physically. Experience teaches us that both the process and the effects of detoxification can positively impact the mind, emotions and soul. There have been many instances when people who suffer from serious illnesses such as cancer, AIDS, allergies, obesity and physical pain have resorted to physical detoxification to gain control over their affliction. What they discovered in the process was that the benefits extended much beyond the physical level.

Holistic detoxification is about the purifying of body, mind as well as soul. It brings with it a greater sense of wholeness. For instance, you cannot feel truly light and free if you are suffering from emotional toxins, no matter how much you fast or sauna. Similarly, however much you meditate to purify spiritually, if your body is full of toxins, from eating, drinking, smoking and abusing substances and you are holding onto old resentments, the benefits of meditation fall short of their potential. There is greater potential for our wholeness and well-being when we make an effort to detoxify all the aspects of our being.

Perhaps emotional detoxification is not as simple as physical detoxification. Emotions are intangible. They are more difficult to control. It is easier to fast or to go for a sauna or massage, but it is far more difficult to control anger and fear. The difficulty with emotions is that they are not easy to reveal even to the expert. In fact, talking about feelings related to trauma, abuse, violence or indeterminate unhappiness could make one feel more guilt. One could end up feeling much worse. The need, therefore, is for a therapy that helps in venting the suppressed emotions. Most experts in the field recommend techniques like breathwork, visualisation, Gestalt psychotherapy and holistic counselling.

Traditionally, people have been brought up to believe that anger and expressing anger are wrong, more so in the case of a woman. As a result there is a suppression of anger. As with any other suppression, over a length of time the emotion will erupt. Many take to replacing the emotions with food obsession, indulgence in alcohol, cigarettes or drugs. The unexpressed anger can accumulate as blocked energy. Suppressed emotions, specifically anger, are widely accepted to be major contributors to depression, clinical stress and all its implications including high blood pressure. When stored anger and guilt about anger are released, we regain energy because it takes energy to suppress emotion.

Aruna, a 47-year-old teacher, was suffering from extreme upper chest pain and constant anxiety when she consulted her doctor. She had difficulty in breathing, which was also shallow in nature. When all attempts at healing failed, she was referred to a psychotherapist. Over a few sessions, Aruna revealed her past grief that related to two major losses, her father and a partner, for whom she had not properly grieved. Since the family had always looked up to her as being strong, she shied away from the process of grieving. She felt that showing emotion was a sign of weakness, so she suppressed her grief and bottled up her feelings.

Aruna was led through a technique of deep breathing and Breathwork. Persistent awareness of deepening her breath helped her to accept and release strong feelings of grief that were locked inside for several years. What began as silent tears were followed by helpless sobbing. Breathing helped her to relax and combat anxiety and allow her to be present with her emotions as they occurred instead of suppressing them by distracting herself. She finally learnt to accept her emotions. The pain in the chest disappeared, and the level of anxiety dropped significantly after a few sessions of the exercise.

The famous author Louise Hay, in her book *You Can Heal Your Life*, admits that repressed anger was a major problem in her cancer healing. Recognising the need for a holistic approach, she also worked on detoxifying her body, using reflexology, special dieting and colon therapy along with therapies to express anger. There is a growing acknowledgment in the medical fraternity that it is necessary to clear underlying suppressed emotions for successful healing of illness.

High self-esteem is fundamental to emotional detoxification. When self-esteem is low, we will deny ourselves the satisfaction of expressing our negative emotions. Unless the toxic belief is made conscious and challenged, it will limit us all through adulthood, negatively influencing our behaviour through fear, self-loathing and guilt.

We have to be willing to challenge our negative self-beliefs constantly to keep the process alive. Our systems simply will not put up with negative suppressed emotion if the positive is allowed to come in strongly and consistently enough. Emotional detoxification can take place successfully when the old emotion is finally allowed to be released. Unlike body detoxification, emotional detoxification is not always a comfortable process, but it is a necessity for healing and well-being.

The power of positive thinking

It is said that you can change your life through the power of positive thinking. Terminal cancer patients have sometimes recovered through this power. When the doctors give up, it is the thought power that can make all the difference. Why else do you think that the doctors stress the cooperation of the patient in healing? Beyond a certain point medicines have no effect, but the mind can aid in healing. It transcends beyond all limits and boundaries and brings about a healing, which has not yet been explained by science.

No one really understands how or why a positive attitude helps people recover faster from surgery or cope better with serious diseases like cancer, heart disease and AIDS. But mounting evidence suggests that these effects may have something to do with the mind's power over the immune system. Some researchers think that pessimism may stress you out, boosting levels of destructive stress hormones in your bloodstream.

What gives rise to negative emotions?

To work on the positive side, one has to first know the causes that give rise to negative emotions. Here are some very common reasons that breed negativity in peoples' minds.

Excessive expectations of what 'should' happen

Clinging on to one negative incident and expecting it to happen all the time

Magnifying your own problems and minimising those of others

Criticising, labelling people instead of their mistakes.

'All or nothing' kind of thinking

Classifying people into 'good' or 'bad'

Emotional reasoning. Exaggerating thinking about the negative consequences of small incidents

Jumping to wrong conclusions

Building a mental filter which harps on one negative incident and ignores the ten positive ones that take place

Blaming yourself for others' mistakes

Disqualifying the positive. Where bad things count, good things don't

Get positive

We have to rid ourselves of toxic emotions for the same reason we must try to recover from a cold before it turns into something deadly like pneumonia. Chronic criticism can often pave the way for arthritis. Guilt seeks for a way to be punished. The tension and stress that fear produces have been cited as suspects in causing baldness, ulcers and high blood pressure. Silently covering up or ignoring toxic emotions year upon year is the major cause of depression. Indeed, the evidence indicates that negative thinking is the root cause of many diseases and illnesses. It can be safely said that criticism, resentment, guilt and fear cause more problems in our bodies and in our lives than anything else. These feelings are the results that come from blaming others and not taking responsibility for our own experiences.

Emotions are nothing but energy in motion and the tremendous burst of energy that comes from an angry tirade can sap a person. Imagine, if you were to use the same energy for a positive action, how much more you would achieve than by simply hurting yourself and others through anger.

I am not saying that you should deny life's darker side or interpret every calamity as a blessing. But when calamity does strike, try not to give in to despair or fatalism. Concluding that you personally have been singled out for suffering, refusing to see any silver lining, and abandoning all hope may not only be a recipe for illness. Such attitudes are also not a great way to go through life. Try to recognise that your grief and pain, however real and deep, are only part of a larger picture, and that this picture includes many elements of pleasure, success and meaning.

Sometimes sufferings bring about a different perspective of life. I once spent a few days in the hospital when I broke my arm. I found that some women exhibited an amazing sense of optimism. Some of them had been operated for cancer and had lost a limb, but they had managed to overcome the obsession with their bodies. As a result, they discovered other interests and talents, such as literature, painting or music.

Remember that even if you can't change the circumstances of your life, you can change your attitude! Just the feeling that you have some say in your own life seems to be good for you – both emotionally and physically. People who don't believe that they have any control over their lives develop a sense of passivity and helplessness, and this sense has been linked to poor health in the same way that feeling loved and hopeful have been linked to better health.

Five positive emotions

Love: Love makes the world go around, no doubts on that score. People in love are happier than those who are not. Love brings warmth, security and happiness. It coheres people. The more you love, the more you get it back.

Hope: The world exists on the foundation of hope. It makes you strong enough to bear the most difficult moments of life. It gives you courage and inspiration. It helps you get up after you have touched the nadir of life. A heart that has no spark of hope in it shrivels up and becomes cold.

Optimism: Do you look for hinges on the doors you open or spot only the rust on them? Optimism is a mind-strengthening emotion. It makes the most difficult situations seem easy.

Kindness: Kindness is the biggest virtue anyone can possess. Whether it is a small kind gesture or a big one, the size of the gesture does not matter. That you have the desire to do your bit to help a person in need is enough. It is the good intention that is needed.

Faith: Whether it is faith in yourself or in God, this one emotion can resolve most of your difficulties. Where there is no faith, miracles cannot occur. Faith can conquer mountains, said the wise, and nothing can be truer.

Express negative emotions

Just as a termite eats in silently into the core of wood, reducing it to worthless powder, negative emotions reduce the human soul into worthless element. They eat into the psyche, ravaging the health and happiness of the person. Why should one want to cling on to negative emotions like anger, frustration, fear or disgust?

At the same time, there is no need for anyone to feel ashamed about the negative emotions that arise in the mind, from time to time. We are neither superhumans nor saints. We are normal human beings who are likely to suffer from various kinds of emotions, some good some bad, at all times. The trick is not to succumb to the negative emotions but gain control over them. To do so, one must understand the power of positive thinking and positive emotions. An unhappy person sees only misery all around him, while a happy person can only detect happiness all around.

For our own well-being and good health, we need to get rid of the negative emotions that cloud our minds. Suppressing emotions can be harmful because these processes require energy, impeding our coping ability, impairing our immune functioning.

Expressing the emotions is better than repressing them, because it allows a flow of truthfulness in the body and spirit. If emotions are very strong, however, expressing them can create both exterior and interior turmoil. The exterior turmoil occurs when we pour our strong emotions all over some unfortunate soul and try to make him or her responsible for our mood. The interior turmoil occurs when we realise we have hurt someone with our outpouring, which makes us feel ashamed of ourselves. Then we either repress the emotions again, or express them even more loudly, neither of which will help anyone.

When we express our emotions, we hand them over to the outside world, where we hope they will be noticed, honoured, healed and transformed into something bright and beautiful. Emotional repression, on the other hand, makes us dependent on the body or the subconscious mind that can only hold so much repressed material before it has to get rid of something. When you hand off your emotional responsibilities to your body, it stores them somewhere until they eventually show up as pain or illness. If you order your subconscious 'No anger or grief, okay?' your unconscious works very hard to obey you, but it has to create something else with all your pent-up anger and grief. So what does it do? It expresses those emotions in some other manner. It represses them and allows them to be manifested as severe bodily pains or mental traumas.

The repression of emotion has serious drawbacks. On the other hand, when you listen to, honour and channel your emotions, you don't need to hand them off to anyone or anything. Emotional channelling lets you handle your emotions yourself. All emotions are messages from our subconscious aspects to our conscious ones. Emotions may spring from our bodies, from our deep memories, or from unused and unnoticed aspects of our psyches. Strong or uncontrollable emotions carry not just truth, but enormous amounts of energy. Strong emotions are the energy warehouse of the soul.

All emotions are tools for our use only if we accept them, channel them responsibly and take the time to listen to their healing messages. Emotional channelling reminds us that a healthy psyche is a complete one. Completeness includes light and dark, good and bad, love and hate, perfection and flaws, solemnity and silliness, wisdom and idiocy, and everything else. If you ignore your own shadowy emotions and try to hide them, or throw them out with the trash, they may loom up and attack you with your own repressed energy. Emotional channelling does not interfere with the expression of our needs, feelings and moods to the aware and supportive people in our lives. Rather, it offers a stronger and more personally-empowering support.

In order to remain normal and human from this moment onwards, you'll need an environment that lets you cry when you're sad, squeal and jump when you're exhilarated, move quickly when you're anxious, protect yourself when you're fearful, stomp and snap when you're angry, dance when you're happy, and grieve when you lose someone or something. Confident people accept and honour all human emotions.

Letting the lachrymals flow

Crying is healthy. Myths about crying being a sign of weakness have been around for such a long time that most people have grown up with the belief that men don't cry; only women and babies do.

There was a time when men would rather be seen dead than with tears in their eyes. But today it is no longer a taboo. Even Bollywood heroes are shown crying on the screen, without any harm to their macho image. In fact, it makes them more human.

Crying is a natural process of catharsis. It brings relief to a burdened and heavy heart. It is an ultimate expression of sadness, and at times, it is also an expression of extreme happiness. Tears can flow unpredictably, when one is touched by a tender gesture. They can mist the eyes when there is relief after excessive tension.

People who are known to be very strong can actually be bottling up a lot of unreleased feelings. Such people are generally more stressed than those who can let the tear ducts get active once in a while.

Says Abhijit, a 35-year-old marketing executive, 'I grew up with the belief that it was unmanly to cry. I didn't ever cry in public, but once in a while I gave vent to my emotions in private. And it brought me great relief. I envy women because they can cry freely.'

It is true that women cry more easily than men. It helps them cope with their emotions much more efficiently than men.

According to Roopa, 'crying is a natural process. I can neither stop myself from crying, nor force myself to cry. I cry when I watch a touching movie, I cry when I am lonely or frustrated. It helps me handle things better.'

It has been observed that people sometimes feel like crying without knowing why they want to cry. It makes them feel better after they have cried for sometime. Acute depression can make a person want to cry. Monday blues can make people cry. Frustrations at work or home can make people cry. The list is endless and so are the benefits.

During Reiki training, we went through a therapy wherein the students were asked to think back into the past, starting from childhood to the present. Loud sobs could be heard as people went back to their early years. Some sobbed inconsolably. Both men and women, strong, sophisticated and eminent, were crying as though there was no tomorrow. At the end of the session, each one of them reported that s/he felt like a new person. All feelings of hurt, sadness and guilt that they had refused to let out for years had suddenly been released.

'I feel so light and refreshed now,' says Anuj. 'I no longer believe in bottling up my emotions. Macho or not macho, I have decided to have a good cry whenever I feel like it.'

I would like to share a very poignant account narrated by a friend. It comes from a man who believed that a crying man is half a man: 'Crying helped me release all the tension, anxiety and frustration of life that had built up inside me. It felt great to relieve myself of all the hurt and pain I was feeling, without being destructive. Crying is a wonderful, intimate experience I would recommend to any man. It's an experience men ought to learn to accept and share with their families. By coming to terms with my own need to cry, I now have a much better understanding of other people's feelings, but most importantly, it has strengthened and enhanced the relationship I now have with my wife and children. Put the macho stuff on hold for a while, guys. Find the strength within yourself to open up your heart and give yourself permission to cry, cry and cry . . . for whatever reason. You'll always come out a better man because of it.'

Psychologist Arun Varma reiterates, 'I would advise everyone to let themselves rid of obsessive emotions. If it is crying that helps them, then let them cry. In fact, I often tell my patients to go through a little bit of silent introspection. They generally come up with the answers themselves.'

Give vent your emotions. Cry to your heart's content and let loose those lachrymals. Tears are nothing to be ashamed of; in fact, they are the best emotional cleansers ever invented. At the end of the cathartic experience, you are sure to feel rejuvenated and refreshed.

RECAP

- ➡ Emotions like anger, resentment, frustration, irritability, bitterness, could cause the liver to malfunction.
- ➡ Although most of us harbour emotional toxins, not many are aware of the harm these toxins can cause.
- ➡ Holistic detoxification is about the purifying of body, mind as well as soul.
- ➡ Suppressed emotions, specifically anger, are widely accepted to be major contributors to depression, clinical stress and all its implications, including high blood pressure.
- ➡ High self-esteem is fundamental to emotional detoxification. When self-esteem is low, we will deny ourselves the satisfaction of expressing our negative emotions.
- ➡ Acceptance and ventilation of negative emotions can help in healing the mind. Emotional channelling is a powerful way to deal with toxic emotions.

SECTION VI

33

DETOXIFYING THE SOUL

Soul is the combined product of mental and emotional energies. A peaceful soul can change the way you perceive things. It can keep us in the highest, most productive, happiest and healthiest mental and emotional state even in the worst of the physical conditions. An enriched soul can bring a lasting sense of peace and joy to a person. A joyful soul can bring about a blissful existence, and if a person is joyful, can good health be far behind? Our mind, body and soul are intrinsically connected to each other, and harmony between these three elements can keep us in a state of optimum well-being.

Over the years we spend on this planet, our souls get jaded and corrupted with the many negative thoughts we harbour in our minds and the materialistic approach we begin to take in our life. This makes it impossible for us to find peace and happiness, or for that matter, relaxation. Toxic thoughts, toxic feelings and emotions prey on the soul causing enough restlessness in us to make us unhealthy. These toxic emotions need to be cleansed, and the soul has to be detoxified before we begin to contemplate a relaxed life.

Don't become so caught up in the effort itself that you lose sight of the reason for it. Always remember that there is a living, feeling, knowing person inside you. One of the most important facts is that life is beautiful. It is a magical gift that has immense possibilities, and we are all here to live it fully. Every day, every hour, every action and every word is an opportunity to add value to life. The more we use these opportunities, the better our lives become.

Healing the soul

What is soul healing? Soul healing is the exploration and application of the true radiant nature of the soul. Soul healing allows one to heal and transcend one's self from the ego to the core of being the Self. In essence, soul healing is a transformation and spiritual journey of the ego en route to the greater, or higher, Self.

In essence, soul healing is a process where you 'become' love. Soul healing allows one to accept full responsibility for his/her own motives, intentions, emotions, desires, thoughts, behaviours and actions. By combining physical, emotional, mental and spiritual realms, soul healing enables persons to discover their collective consciousness and bring forth harmony.

Soul healing unlocks barriers that have essentially held a person back. Soul healing helps you to discover past lives, personal essence and energetically clears chakras and meridian points. Soul healing also helps discover the symbols that unlock past information, as well as discovery of one's mission and purpose in life. Soul healing can release energetic patterns from past traumas, karmic attachments, inter-connection with God and much more.

When our bodies become poisoned, whether from alcohol or drugs or environmental toxins, we must go through a detoxification process to regain health. Similarly, when the soul has suffered from the poisonous ill effects of our thoughts, it needs to be healed and detoxified.

Just as our bodies can be weakened by exposure to poisons, our minds are susceptible to the toxins of craving, aversion and ignorance. These mental toxins arise naturally in human life, and unfortunately, our culture often encourages them. Most of us live in a toxic soup of fear, anger, envy and impatience. Just as the addict indulges in unhealthy behaviour that, for a while, masks the nature of the poison, we delude ourselves into thinking that material things and sensual pleasures can remove our unhappiness. Happiness arises naturally when we become free of the mental and emotional toxins that poison us.

Meditation is a tool we can use to detoxify the mind. When we meditate, we suspend our indulgence in toxic thoughts. When we open the mind and just observe, we can begin to see the source of our difficulties.

When we quieten the mind, we can see the source of our misery in our toxic memories and thoughts. We may find that sitting still stimulates the flow of negative thoughts and emotions. Just as an alcoholic in detox may experience shakiness, hallucinations and unpleasant body sensations, when we attempt to still the mind, the mental impurities may manifest themselves. This is the opportunity to go beyond our addiction to them and observe them at their source. The sources of misery are not outside us. They are within the structure of the body/mind. In the peace of a quieter mind we can see the truth.

The word 'meditation' means different things to different people. There are hundreds of different schools of meditation, many associated with some form of religious practice and many that are not. Some of these varied forms of meditation may include techniques such as complex visualisation or chanting words or sounds known as 'mantras'. Meditation is a truly holistic activity in that, ideally, the whole system of body, mind and spirit is involved and benefited. It is one of the greatest methods to unwind, relax the mind and trigger the body's own natural relaxation response.

It is the practice of concentrating on an object, word or idea to clear the mind, relax the body and achieve a state of heightened awareness and enlightenment. Meditation has been a feature of many religions, but it can also serve as a practical, calming therapy. It cuts off the sensory input, halts the demands of the brain, and gives the mind a chance to rest. Research projects have shown that meditation can lower blood pressure, reduce the body's metabolic rate and ameliorate many stress-related disorders.

Physical benefits

The physical benefits of meditation include relaxation, improvement of sleeping patterns, lowering of high blood pressure, recovery from fatigue and general beneficial effect on most stress-related diseases. Meditation slows down the rate of breathing, helps the muscles relax, gives the body time to eliminate lactic acid and other waste products, reduces anxiety and reduces stress headaches.

Awareness of the body is an essential part of effective meditation. Many of the emotional stresses and upsets that people experience can be held as tensions in the body and therefore be fairly unconscious. Through the process of conscious relaxation of body and breathing that meditation entails, these stresses can be unlocked from their hiding places in the muscles and joints and released.

Meditation fortifies the immune system and promotes physical health. The Alpha and Theta brainwaves lower the blood pressure and the pulse rate. It is an excellent remedy for insomnia and other stress-related ailments. With the meditative state of mind come the factors like self-healing of the mind as well as the body.

Mental benefits

Meditation teaches one to fix his mind more firmly in the present reality, to have accurate and easy recall to lead a more wholesome, happy, healthy and meaningful life. It eliminates stressful thoughts and promotes clear thinking. It also helps sharpen focus and concentration. It also reduces irritability.

Meditation can improve the ability to concentrate, the ability to listen, both to others and yourself. Although people cannot change their external conditions to any large extent, they can take the responsibility of changing their attitudes and reactions, the way the mind interacts with the world. One of the most effective and safest ways to bring about this change is to meditate.

The path of meditation offers a way of becoming more aware and alive to every aspect, inner and outer. The practice known as 'mindfulness' is simply carrying this present-centred attention into one's daily life and activities, whether walking or running or doing household chores.

Spiritual benefits

With meditation a whole new realm is unravelled to the mind. It promotes a spiritualistic thinking, which brings inner peace to an individual.

Meditation

Meditation is very useful if:

You have been under long term stress

You have been under short term stress, which has caused adrenaline to be released into your bloodstream

You have been worrying about problems

You have been physically active

The posture, place and practice

'How often should I practise?' 'How should I sit?' These are the questions often asked by those starting out on the path of meditation. For both these questions there are no 'right' answers, no specific way of meditating. Individuals explore for themselves, evolving an effective and appropriate practice. As for time and frequency, some schools suggests many hours a day, some advocate quality rather than quantity, a short focused period of meditation of five or ten minutes.

Meditation seems to work best when the spine is straight, but relaxed and vertical. There are several reasons for this. First, sitting upright is a very good way of staying awake and alert while the eyes are closed and the attention drawn inwards. If the body is upright, the breath can move in and out freely without obstruction. Also the muscles of the torso and spine have a chance to unknot themselves of tensions.

Sitting upright sends a message to the unconscious that although your eyes are closed; you are not going to sleep, as you would when lying down. On a more subtle level, the body's prana energy, or life force, is able to move more freely if the spine is straight. Energy cannot move through tense muscles, so a relaxed way of sitting needs to be found.

If you find it difficult to sit on the floor, sitting in a chair is also acceptable. If sitting cross-legged on the floor, you will probably find it helpful to have a firm cushion at least 2–3 inches thick, under your bottom. This lifts the spine so that it is easier to sit upright. You may choose to kneel, in which case, sitting on a larger cushion or a meditation bench would be advisable to prevent cutting off circulation to the legs. If you feel most comfortable sitting in a chair, choose one that is the right height for you. A firm, straight-backed chair is better than an armchair and if you can sit up unsupported, it is still better.

Focusing

Your breath also provides an ever-present and easily-accessible focus for concentration. One is always breathing! Many schools of meditation like Vipassana, teach how to focus on the breath in various ways.

This may involve imagining that the breath originates in one particular point of the body. The points most usually focused on are the *hara* or *tan tien* – just below and behind the navel, or the heart, in the centre of the chest. The crown of the head, the base of the spine or the soles of the feet may all be included in the awareness. Focusing on the breath can also take the form of noticing the physical changes as the breath moves in and out, either at the nostrils or the abdomen. Meditation can be as simple as this, just breathing while sitting.

The Buddhist way of meditation based on the breath technique is called *anapana.* It involves watching the in-going and out-going breath and being conscious of the process. You have to move mentally with the breath and observe the inhalation and exhalation. You can meditate anytime and anywhere if you learn the art of mindfulness. Mindfulness is a Zen meditation technique in which full focus is given to the present. Make a conscious effort to practise it. If you are chopping vegetables, empty your mind of everything else; focus on the act of chopping, the colours of the foods, their aromas. Love the sensation of being fully engaged with the world around you.

A simple form of meditating

Sit upright with erect spine and closed or downcast eyes. Concentrate on your respiration. Notice your in-breath and your out-breath. Don't try to change your breathing. Just watch the breath flow in and out.

As you observe your breath, memories, thoughts and feelings may arise. Notice them, but don't cling to them. Don't try to make them go away. Just observe them dispassionately and let them go. Continue to follow your breath and stay awake and aware.

As thoughts and emotions arise, observe how they arise. How do they come to you? As discomfort arises, observe how it arises. What is the source of the discomfort?

Use this quiet time to learn about yourself. Allow the impurities of the mind to arise and dissipate. Be patient. Sit in the light of true self-healing and experience the truth beyond mind and matter.

Meditation with imagery

When meditation is combined with imagery, it can bring about a total rejuvenating experience. All you have to do is to create a mental image of a pleasant and relaxing place in your mind. Involve all your senses in the imagery: see the place, hear the sounds, smell the aromas, feel the temperature and the movement of the wind. Enjoy the location in your mind.

In all cases it is important to keep your attention focused. If external thoughts or distractions wander in, let them drift out. If necessary, visualise attaching the thoughts to objects and then move the objects out of your attention.

Some time back, while travelling in the train, I came across a Korean master who was teaching a new concept in meditation called smile meditation. We spoke about this therapy in great details. He told me that smile meditation advocates using the inner smile for calming the mind. The next time you notice yourself feeling tense or stressed, try the technique of the 'inner smile'. In ancient Chinese medicine a similar approach to this is said to activate the *tan tien*, the energy store of your body, just below our navel. Laughter therapy is based on the same principle and the effectiveness of a good belly laugh is also dependent on the activation of the *tan tien.*

After I returned from the trip, I decided to try out the technique of inner smile and was pleasantly surprised to note that it worked very well indeed. It had a sort of lightening effect on my heart and generated a pleasant kind of warmth inside. Think of something that makes you feel happy: this could be the smell of freshly-baked cake or a joyful moment from your past – anything that brings a smile in your heart. Allow this smile to travel within you until it sits in your abdomen radiating warmth throughout the body. A refreshing feeling of lightness and happiness covers the mind after you have enjoyed the inner smile. It actually keeps you happy and smiling through the day.

Smile meditation

Smile meditation is based on Taoist meditation practice. In this kind of meditation, we have to use the smile that we give others for our own good. The inner smile is an opportunity to offer a smile to oneself. It can be done in a seated meditation session or in the midst of daily life.

To begin with, find a comfortable posture for meditation (seated on a cushion or blanket, in a chair, or against a wall). It may be helpful to set a timer for 10, 20 or 30 minutes, so you can sink deeply into your meditation without wondering about the time.

Place your hands on your knees in *Jnana Mudra* (index and thumb touching), with palms facing up to open your awareness or palms facing down to calm the mind. Do a body scan and relax any tension you may be holding. Let your spine rise from the root of the pelvis. Draw your chin slightly down and lengthen the back of your neck.

Begin by generating a feeling of natural happiness as if it emanates from the backs of the eyes. If the feeling does not come naturally, remind yourself of any experience of natural joy – for example, the face of a joyous child. You can use any past experience of happiness to lighten up your face and bring a smile.

Once you generate the feeling of this smile, let it radiate down the backs of your eyes like a waterfall. Visualise this meditative stream flowing down the centre of your spine, to your heart and lungs, then into your stomach and spleen (under your left lower ribs), and liver (under your right lower ribs). Let it run down through the kidneys (back ribs), the colon and intestines (belly), down into your genitals, and out into your legs and feet.

You can repeat the sweep from the backs of the eyes to the feet or do one long, slow sweep. The inner smile can be its own complete meditation, or it may lead you into an effortless meditative absorption.

Remain in this happy position for as long as you wish. When you have finished, bring your hands together and complete your meditation with a moment of gratitude, reflection or prayer to seal the energy of your meditation into your life. Remember that you can cultivate the inner smile anytime throughout the day to fill the heart with compassion.

RECAP

- Soul is the combined product of mental and emotional energies. A peaceful soul can change the way we perceive things.
- Toxic thoughts and emotions prey on the soul causing enough restlessness in us to make us unhealthy.
- Toxic emotions need to be cleansed, and the soul has to be detoxified before we begin to contemplate a relaxed life.
- Life is beautiful. It is a magical gift that has immense possibilities, and we are all here to live it fully.
- Soul healing is the exploration and application of the true radiant nature of the soul.
- Soul healing is a transformation and spiritual journey of the ego en route to the greater, or higher, Self.
- Meditation is a tool we can use to detoxify the mind. When we meditate, we suspend our indulgence in toxic thoughts. When we open the mind and just observe, we can begin to see the source of our difficulties.
- Meditation is a holistic activity in which the whole system of body, mind and spirit is involved and

benefited. It is one of the greatest methods to unwind, relax the mind and trigger the body's own natural relaxation response.

34

ALTERING THE MIND MAP

We live in a sea of vibrations of different frequencies – both negative and positive. We cannot change things around us, but we can change ourselves to consciously flow with the tide. The mind is a very complex thing. It makes us react to different situations in many different ways, on different occasions. Not all of our reactions are based on the dictates of our conscious. Many of them are triggered by the feelings of 'ego' that exist within us. We are all riding on a superfast train called 'Ego Express', which is bound for one destination that is the 'I', 'Me', 'Myself' land. We are so lost in our sense of 'I' that we don't want to reach any other destination.

There are several effective ways to change the way we perceive the world. One of the most powerful tools of mind management and detoxification of the soul is regular prayers. They are immensely powerful tools of healing. Earlier, it was only godmen and the gurus who advocated prayers in one's daily routine, but now the doctors are also suggesting that a regular prayer session could save your heart from falling prey to fatal diseases.

In a study conducted in 1997, it was found that Indians who prayed regularly were 70 per cent less likely to suffer from heart disease than those who didn't follow the daily prayer routine.

Prayers and meditations have been an inherent discipline in the life of Indians in the past. In fact, the connection between body and soul has existed in our culture for centuries. This connection was used by healers to cure people of most diseases, but with advancement of science and medicine, the importance of the mind–body connection was ignored by most healers and doctors. We began following the western practitioners in our healing practices. As we progressed, we lost the vital wisdom that was followed by our sages and healers. The natural herbs and medicines were replaced with antibiotics and western prescriptions. The resultant reactions to the antibiotics were discovered much later.

Prayers are a potent power that helps us cope with all kinds of adversities and negative forces in our lives. They are the salvation for depressed and hopeless beings.

The importance of the eastern medicine and cures was rediscovered by us only when the western world, after suffering from the ill effects of their own medicine, woke up and acclaimed them. All of a sudden, there was clamour for all kinds of ancient eastern wisdom; from yoga to Ayurveda and religion, everything was rediscovered by the Indians.

Praying has been a part of every Indian household for centuries. Thankfully, the practice of praying every evening is still followed by most families. With more evidence coming our way about the efficacy of prayers in healthy living, it is imperative that the younger generation be taught the benefits of following the footsteps of the older generations.

For several years, scientists and doctors have been researching on the link between prayers and a healthy life. Spiritual support groups have sprung up in the western countries to help the ailing people, especially the terminally ill. Tremendous recovery in some patients points to the power of prayers. The positive energy that is generated during the prayers has certainly a much more powerful effect than the scientists realise. We have just been exposed to the tip of the iceberg; the immense potentiality of praying has yet to be discovered. Today, there are more than a hundred medical colleges in the United States, which have a course called Religious Traditions in Health Care. This subject is taught to the medical students and covers the correlation between spirituality and health. It also teaches about the major religions across the globe from a medical perspective.

Researchers are slowly unravelling the deep connection between spirituality and our body, through painstaking research. Some of the astounding facts that have been unveiled by them are:

Healthier Level of Blood Pressure: In a path-breaking finding, researchers found significant protective effects against high BP in men who are religious and pray regularly. One of the explanations could be that all activities that control stress are good for the heart and both prayers as well as chanting have a soothing effect on the mind. We suffer from high blood pressure because of the disturbed mind, and when the same mind is calm, during prayers, it brings a healing effect on the heart and all blood vessels.

General Sense of Well-Being and Happiness: Epidemiologist and author Jeff Levin conducted a study on old people and discovered that the old adults who are religious have fewer health problems and a better sense of well-being than those who were not religious. Well-being, again, depends on the state of our minds and souls. If the mind is calm and the soul satisfied, the physical benefits will definitely be available.

Recuperative Power: In a study conducted at the Dartmouth Medicine School, doctors found that patients who had gone through open-heart surgery and who were religious had three times the chance of being alive after the first six months of surgery. Faith brings healing, and when people have faith in their healer and the supreme, they were more likely to survive the surgery and other medical problems than those who were sceptical.

Sturdy Hearts: In a study conducted in 1997, it was found that Hindus who prayed regularly were 70 per cent less likely to have coronary heart disease. In Hindu belief, the heart is not just an organ for pumping blood, but also a compassionate and religious organ. We tend to involve emotions with the heart. A religious heart with positive emotions is, therefore, more likely to remain healthy.

Longer Life Expectancy: Studies show a seven year difference between life expectancy of the believers and the non-believers.

Reduced Emotional and Psychological Ailments: Those who pray regularly are less likely to suffer from psychological and emotional problems like depression and anxiety. This could be due to several facts. One of them is the deep involvement with religion, which brings a sense of security to the person. this is especially true when people go through group religious practices like satsang and kirtan sessions where the group therapy works on a mental level.

De-stressing and Enhanced Immunity Benefits: Dr Herbert Benson of Harvard Medical School found that practices like meditation, prayer, *tai chi* and yoga reduce stress and enhances immunity. We all know that most ailments are related to the high levels of stress that people are going through in modern times. Stress brings with it a lowered immunity level, besides the heart problems and other ailments. Prayer, yoga and meditation are very potent methods of de-stressing. Hence, they bring with them the allied health benefits.

But the prayer as we know it is just another means of asking for more from God. We get on our knees and beg for something; we do charity and ask for our wishes to be granted; we go to temples and ask for favours. That is not all, we promise to bribe God when the wish gets fulfilled. We tell God, 'Oh, God, let me get a good job, and I will donate Rs. 501 to your temple', or some such equally ridiculous thing. We trudge long distances when someone tells us about a temple, which houses a powerful deity who grants all kinds of boons.

This is not prayer. Prayers should be meant as genuine thanks-giving to God for having gifted us with precious life. It should be meant as praise to the Almighty for giving us the little things that we take for granted. Only then can it bring peace and happiness to us. Or else, it remains a futile exercise. A true prayer is an outpouring from the heart, not of emotionalism but of intense joy and thanksgiving. It can happen anywhere, anytime, and wherever it happens, that moment is sacredness beyond compare. Prayer is a feeing of gratitude when you enjoy the beauty of nature. It is the cry of the heart when one sees the suffering of another. True prayer is when you attune yourself with the infinite. Prayer is a feeling from a heart in harmony.

RECAP

- Astute philosophical and spiritual teachers such as Plato, Christ and Buddha told us that what we focus upon eventually becomes part of our existence.
- This concept, once dismissed as religious or metaphysical superstition, is now being proven by such scientific disciplines as quantum physics and neurobiology.
- Toxic thought patterns lead to various forms of self-destructive behaviour, including the creation and retention of regrets that burden us.
- Negative, angry, sad and self-defacing thoughts are toxic to your system. These poisons activate neuro-physiological responses within the body. These, when combined with other contributory factors, lead to the manifestations of diseases such as cancer, allergies, immune deficiencies, headaches and colitis.
- Within the mind this toxicity can cause depression, anxiety, worry and a sense of abandonment within the spirit.
- Prayers are a potent power that helps us cope with all kinds of adversities and negative forces in our lives.

35

THE ART OF FORGIVING

'Forgiveness is the fragrance the violet releases when it is crushed upon.'
—Mark Twain

How often have we found ourselves saying 'I will never forgive you for this'? Many times, I am sure. Right from our school days when we felt let down by a friend to the present day when we feel let down by the spouse, whether in our careers or personal life, the unforgiving stance is a common occurrence. We brood over the so-called wrongs committed by the people we trust and promise not to forget or forgive.

Nothing causes more stress and diminished output than the grudge we harbour against someone. It is our fault-finding and condemning others as well as ourselves that not only causes us stress but also has the potential of being injurious to our health. The grievances that we carry with us from old and new personal relationships can play a significant role in many of our illnesses.

Today, if there were a new medicine in the market which promised to get rid of our different body aches, insomnia, and other problems, free of cost and without any side effects, we would all rush to buy it by the dozen. We would conveniently forget that most of these psychosomatic diseases are caused by anger, grievances, guilt and shame. We would forget that all these ailments that are frequently caused by our angry emotions and unforgiving thoughts.

Here is a ready-made panacea gifted by God. One which costs nothing, has no side effects and works like a miracle but which we are not willing to use. Forgiveness, the miracle, cure, is available to all who want to exercise it. Besides mopping up all the ailments, it would gift us with a healthy and happy mind, totally guilt-free. As a bonus we would be granted the physical fitness to go with it.

Holding on to grievances and unforgiving thoughts is like putting toxins into the mind. While none of us would consciously swallow poison, we continue to keep angry, toxic thoughts in our minds, which are lethal to our systems. Our emotions affect our immune system and every organ in the body. Holding on to bitterness and resentment is like slow poisoning.

Mounting evidence now suggests that not forgiving others may get you gallstones; if the problem pertains to the spouse, the stones form in the kidneys instead. The ensuing emotions and anger may involve back problems depending on whether the lack you feel is in emotional or material support.

If you have unrealistically high standards of judgment, which make it difficult for you to forgive, your nagging nature may give rise to complicated medical problems relating to liver and other digestive organs.

A gentle word, a kind gesture, one kind thought could open up a new world for you. Unlike what many people believe, forgiveness is not submission but a rational way to growth. It doesn't indicate weakness but strengths. It brings the world closer to you, forges better bonds. It strengthens your mind, body and soul, which need to be purged of all negativity.

When we make the decision not to forgive, we are actually deciding to continue suffering. Why then do so many of us find it so difficult to forgive? When we forgive someone, it does not mean that we support the things he did. Forgiveness simply means that we have made the decision to heal our own minds by letting go of the hurtful past, a past that our anger and judgments cannot change.

My friend Sharad Rathore once narrated an incident to me. He had not spoken to his stepmother for years because he harboured a resentment against her for having replaced his mother's rightful place. Neither did he visit his father. He instigated the other siblings and did everything possible to make life difficult for them. For years, he avoided attending family functions and kept himself aloof from all ties. The simmering anger within him began to take a toll on his mental and physical health. Sharad knew that he had to bridge the differences with his family, but his ego prevented him from doing so.

It was on his daughter's betrothal that he realised that he wanted his father's blessings for her. Sharad personally went with the invitation to his father and begged for forgiveness. His father hugged him lovingly and they patched up the differences.

Forgiveness is the bridge to love, peace, happiness and well-being. It allows us to cleanse our souls of guilt, blame and shame. When we forgive, we transcend the barriers of ego and pompousness. We connect with that which is greater than our self and become better human beings. Nursing resentments turn us into shallow people.

Anita Kapoor is an example of how toxic thoughts affect the body. Five years ago, her husband was murdered by a business associate, who was convicted of the murder and sentenced to prison for life. Anita was not satisfied with the sentence. She believed that he had committed an unforgivable act and should have got a death sentence. She fought the case to the High Court. In the process she spent more money than she had budgeted for; she also squandered more precious energy and time than she could afford. She wanted revenge at all cost. The rage she harboured engulfed her mind.

Through the years, Anita developed an increasing number of medical problems. She lost her glorious hair, developed stones in the gall bladder, and suffered from asthmatic and digestive problems. This was not all. When the High Court turned down her appeal, she began to suffer from acute depression and neurotic state of mind, which required her to undergo psychotherapy.

It was during this phase that Anita met a spiritual teacher. She attended several workshops and realised that it was time she let go of her anger and vengeful thoughts, for her own good. On the suggestion of her spiritual guru, she made a symbolic gesture of forgiveness. By continued affirmations of her forgiveness, she was eventually able to recover from most of her ailments.

A look into the lives of saints would educate us on the value of forgiveness. There was a woman who always abused and threw garbage on Prophet Mohammed whenever he passed her house. One day, while passing her house, the Prophet was surprised when she did not hurl abuses or throw garbage at him. He climbed up the steps of her house to inquire about the health and well-being of the lady. His act of compassion and forgiveness brought an intense sense of remorse in the woman, who immediately became his follower.

It is tough to forgive

We are not Prophet Mohammed, and so it is difficult for most of us to forgive the people who have harmed us. Forgiveness is tough because of:

He climbed up the steps of her house to enquire about the health and well being of the lady.

Vengeful Thoughts: We carry thoughts of hatred because we blame others for the bad that befalls us. This illusion seems comforting. It does not require us to take any responsibility and allows us to judge others without letting ourselves be judged. It gives us a chance to become the object of sympathy and earn approval of others.

Fear of Being Mistaken: We fear that the other person may continue with his unwanted and irrational behaviour if we forgive. It is a baseless fear. There are more chances of a person understanding the foolishness of his action in the calm waters of forgiving silence than in the disturbed state of reactive behaviour. Your hatred, on the other hand, may make his behaviour look justified to him. So, if you really want him to change, practise forgiveness.

Programmed Behaviour: We expect others to behave the way we want. This may be unreasonable, but it can actually happen without any resistance, provided we surrender the desire and let people behave the way they have learnt to behave and let things happen the way they are bound to happen. We should be grateful to the universe for all that is happening to us. This is what is programmed in our best interests.

Grudges and Resentments: We continue to hold grudges against the people we presume to have wronged us. We refuse to accept that all that is happening to us is a result of the seeds sown by us, the way we process the behaviour of others and respond to any stimuli that we are exposed to. No one else is responsible for our unpleasant experiences. Our distress at others' behaviour reflects our own inner turmoil.

Labels: The fear of being labelled as weak, dumb and timid often stops us from forgiving. We think forgiveness is an excuse for escapism, inaction or cowardice and only those who cannot fight believe in forgiving. But there is an obvious difference between fearing and forgiving. Yes, there are people who disguise their fears as forgiveness. But your decision to forgive will not turn you into a coward. Moreover, why should we be ashamed of admitting that we cannot fight?

Tips on forgiveness

Forgiveness becomes easy when we recognise that it is an act of strength, not weakness. When we forgive, it elevates us to a higher level of spirituality.

When we continue to hold on to grievances and unforgiving thoughts, we are choosing to suffer. Rising above the level of self-pity can make it easier to forgive. When we begin to delight in holding on to the grudges, we also allow the soul to decay.

Past events cannot hurt us, but holding on to the thoughts about the past can cause immense distress and pain. Pain and distress are caused because we hold on to the memories of the past. Anger and judgments can't change the past or punish someone else, but they can hurt us.

It is no coincidence that the happiest people are those who choose not to judge and know the value of forgiveness.

Ask yourself this question, 'Does holding on to my justified anger really bring me peace of mind?' Anger and peace, judgment and happiness do not occur at the same time. Will holding on to anger bring us what we want? When you carry on with your grudges, you not only allow the other person to hurt you, but also let him control your life each moment you are affected by his thoughts.

It becomes much easier to forgive when we realise that angry, unhappy thoughts about the past are poisoning our life. Forgiveness is an act of kindness to ourselves because there is no point in punishing ourselves for someone else's foolishness.

The best way to stop thinking about a past event is to accept your past and embrace the present. Forgiving the wrongdoings and wrongdoer erases the wrong and lightens the soul.

Choose to be happy rather than right. When we stop trying to control others and focus instead on our own thoughts, we gift our soul with freedom and peace, which eventually lead to well-being.

We give ourselves the greatest gift when we choose loving thoughts over angry ones. Your mind is not a dustbin that will remain unaffected by the trash you put into it. Treat it like a garden, and it will blossom. Everyone has the power to choose the thoughts he puts into the mind.

Forgiveness is the key to true happiness. There is enough chaos around us, and to remain happy we have to clear the chaos in our minds. Wisdom dictates that we do not let external circumstances or people decide whether we will be happy. Anger, judgments and unforgiving thoughts make us suffer; similarly, releasing them brings us joy.

By forgiving we harmonise ourselves with the greater truth and cosmic energies around us. It drives out the negative energy replacing it with the positive.

The mere act of forgiveness makes us grow as spiritual souls, pushing us towards our liberation. Even when we win a rat race, we remain rats but the act of forgiving makes us rise above that level.

RECAP

- Nothing causes more stress and diminished output than the grudge we harbour against someone.
- Holding on to bitterness and resentment is like slow poisoning.
- Mounting evidence now suggests that not forgiving others may get you gallstones.
- Nagging nature may give rise to complicated medical problems relating to liver and other digestive organs.
- Forgiveness is not submission but a rational way to growth.
- Forgiveness simply means that we have made the decision to heal our own minds by letting go of the hurtful past, a past that our anger and judgments cannot change.
- By forgiving we harmonise ourselves with the greater truth and cosmic energies around us. It drives out the negative energy replacing it with the positive.

36

A MENTAL DETOXIFICATION TECHNIQUE

Combining visualisation with colour therapy can be one of the most powerful techniques in relaxing both the mind and the soul. I found this technique to work excellently in times of intense distress. This technique can be used to heal the mind through colour cleansing of chakras.

A word about chakras

Chakras are the seven main energy centres of the body, and aura is our energy field, which some gifted individuals claim to see as a haze of coloured light surrounding the body. The colours in the aura have their own significance and are affected by our health and energy quality. It has been found that the aura of bodies, when exposed to colour therapy, alter their effect dramatically. They trigger a series of changes in the systems, organs and cells. Before you discard the importance of aura and chakras, let me tell you that scientific research and Kirlian photography have proved the existence of an aura around every earthly object. Most health experts have long accepted the power of the chakras, which are considered potent elements that influence our health and well-being.

The six nerve centres, seven major chakras and many subsidiary chakras can be influenced through chromotherapy. The chakras are stationed along the central axis of your being. Each one is a point at which energy can be expressed in a certain set of actions, attitudes and emotions. The chakras are a map of the soul, along which you must move for healing to occur. These points represent our physical, mental, emotional and spiritual growth. When these points are healthy and in balance, we remain in peak health.

The chakras are bell-shaped vortices, which are the whirling centres of power. Each of them is associated with a specific colour, and these colours have a healing effect and energising effect on the chakra and the organs controlled by them. Each of the chakras spins at a varying rate producing far-reaching effects on the body.

The combined power of chakras, colour and visualisation can work in an amazing manner to bring comfort and a tranquillising effect on the brain. This is how you do it:

Select a quiet room with no disturbing sounds. It should be cool and comfortable.

Lie on a mat on the ground, and close your eyes.

Let the body muscles relax slowly, starting from the toes to the head. Become aware of each muscle and loosen it wilfully. Continue this exercise till you begin to feel totally relaxed.

Now concentrate on your breath. Sense your breath moving in and out of your nostrils.

As you concentrate, you will be able to feel the warmth of the exhaled air and the coolness of the inhaled air.

At this juncture you should be able to hear your heartbeats and feel the working of your heart.

Visualise yourself at the beach with the rolling of blue waves around you. You are lying on the golden sands with palm fronds waving above you. All around you is a beautiful forest of green trees. Waves from the sea are touching your toes, and you can feel the cool breeze fanning your body.

As the scenery becomes almost real, focus on your heart chakra and feel it spinning with great energy. Visualise it being surrounded by a giant, green, glowing orb, washing the chakra lovingly.

As you visualise the chakra being tended by the loving hands of the green colour, you will feel peace descending on your mind.

Shift your focus to the throat chakra. A lump will rise at that part of your body as you shift your attention to it. Visualise a blue satin material enveloping the throat in a loving manner, wiping away all impurities from it. It is awash with a soft blue light, purifying and soothing.

As the throat is washed clean of all stress and worries, focus your attention on the Ajna chakra, which lies between your brows. This is the seat of your third eye, a powerful energy emanates from this region. The Ajna chakra energy has much to do with the emotional intelligence and clears all kinds of emotional confusion.

The third eye is guided by the colour indigo, so envelop the seat of this chakra with this colour to bring tranquillity and peace to your soul. Imagine the indigo flame with its cool and luminescent light radiating all around the Ajna chakra.

As the third eye is cleansed of all stress, move up to the crown chakra. This is the most powerful chakra, associated with spirituality, divinity and super consciousness. It guides the mind into the path of wisdom, bliss and spiritual power. The colour violet is associated with crown chakra, and this is the colour that you must visualise as you focus your attention on the sahasrara chakra. See the soothing, soft, petals of violet flower caressing your crown, bringing a sensation of comfort, calm and placid contentment to your being.

Lastly, let the feelings of calmness flow through you as you inhale deeply.

When done properly, this exercise will rejuvenate and refresh your entire body, mind and soul. It should recharge your energy and dispel all stress and fatigue.

37

HOLISTIC DETOXIFICATION GUIDE

It is possible that reading through all the therapies for detoxification, you could be confused about the one that you need to follow. It is best to adhere to a plan that is both simple and inexpensive to follow. Here is a plan that I recommend and can safely vouch for its effectivity since I practise it myself:

To Detoxify	Therapy	Duration	Frequency
Digestive system	Vegetarianism	-	All meals
	Fasting with fruit juices	24 hours	Weekly
Lymphatic system	Body brushing	-	Weekly
	Massage	20 minutes	Monthly
Respiratory system	Pranayama	20 minutes	Daily
Excretory system	2 litres of water and lots of fibre.	-	Daily
All systems	Yoga and walking	30 minutes	Daily
The mind	Meditation/chakra cleansing	15 minutes	Daily
	Shavasana	5 minutes	Daily
The soul	Affirmations and prayers	15 minutes	Daily

A true detox regimen should include taking time out of your day, every day, to relax and reflect. Make a mental list of factors in your life that are 'toxic' and list out the steps you can take to eliminate them.

Post-detox maintenance regimen

A healthy post-detox lifestyle also includes following a daily routine to rejuvenate inside and out by engaging in activities that are relaxing as well as stimulating. A regular regimen of exercise such as yoga, meditation, aromatherapy (either in the form of candles or in baths), therapeutic massage and a quiet period for introspection, are all integral steps for achieving lasting health and wellness.

One of the prime causes of a toxic body is diet. It is hard to avoid toxins found in the air and in water, but we can do much to eliminate them from our diets. To improve your diet, eat less of some foods and more of others.

Processed sugar and flour, processed foods and other 'junk foods' should be eliminated. Processed foods contain many additives and sweeteners, which can be toxic, and overly refined foods can 'get stuck' in the intestinal tract, forming a sort of 'papier-mache' crust within. Needless to say, this makes it difficult for nutrients to be absorbed. This crust also slows down transit time – the time from ingestion to excretion. This is important, because the longer partially-digested food stays in the body, the better chance there is that carcinogens and toxins will be absorbed.

Eat less meat, as meat is more difficult to digest and contains unhealthy fat. It also may contain xenoestrogens (foreign estrogens) as a result of animal growth hormone shots. Eat more raw fruits and vegetables. They supply live enzymes, which ensure you get more nutritional benefits. The enzymes found in raw foods help the body's digestive enzymes break down the foods we eat to free up the nutrients within. Helping the body's digestive enzymes means they do not have to work as hard, which frees up energy for other important tasks.

After the age of 40, levels of digestive enzymes begin to decrease. This means you do not digest food as well as you might, which can result in getting less nutrition, but also in more waste material remaining in the digestive tract. This, in turn, leads to accumulation of toxic elements in the body.

After detoxification, a maintenance programme can help in keeping the systems working in peak order. Here are some useful guidelines on maintaining a toxin-free body:

Eat plenty of fibre, including brown rice and organically grown fresh fruits and vegetables. Beets, radishes, artichokes, cabbage, broccoli, spirulina, chlorella and seaweed are excellent detoxifying foods.

Cleanse and protect the liver by taking herbs such as dandelion root, burdock and milk thistle, and drinking green tea.

Take vitamin C, which helps the body produce glutathione, a liver compound that drives away toxins.

Reduce sugar intake. A recent study at New York State University in Buffalo documented that within two hours of eating 300 calories of sugar, the number of free radicals increased by 140 per cent. Experts say that consumption should never exceed more than 40 grams of sugar a day.

Avoid alcohol, caffeine, and nicotine.

Drink at least two litres of water daily.

Breathe deeply to allow oxygen to circulate more completely through your system.

Transform stress by emphasising positive emotions.

Practise hydrotherapy by taking a very hot shower for five minutes, allowing the water to run on your back. Follow with cold water for 30 seconds. Do this three times, and then get into bed for 30 minutes.

Sweat in a sauna, so your body can eliminate wastes through perspiration.

Dry-brush your skin to remove toxins through your pores.

Exercise: Two forms of exercise are particularly beneficial in detoxifying the body. Aerobic exercise supports detox by encouraging sweating, increasing circulation, breaking down fat and stimulating the lymphatic system.

Yoga aids the detox process by stretching the muscles and releasing the toxins. It teaches proper breathing, balances inner body energy, and stimulates the lymphatic system.

A 20-minute yoga session, at least three times a week is very beneficial in detoxification.

Cut out the stress.The top 10 stress fighters:

Plan ahead: Manage your time and your duties.

Cut down on caffeine: Get your lift from ginger and peppermint teas, which boost energy and mental clarity.

Practise yoga: Even gentle stretching every day is beneficial.

B Vitamins: Include breakfast cereals, whole grain bread, milk, meat, yogurt, eggs, and bananas.

Release tension during the day: Plan periodic tension release sessions.

Eat carbohydrates for lunch: one and a half to two ounces of bread, pasta, rice, or potato .

Exercise: Just 10 minutes of walking a day helps detox.

Aromatherapy: 15 minutes daily provides a calm psychological tension reducer.

Supplement your adrenal glands: Ginseng is the most

commonly recommended 'booster' in a dose of 500 to 1,000 mg per day .

Good sleep: Milk or dairy products and protein contain tryptophan, which helps deep sleep.

Take a sauna: The human immune system works better at slightly higher temperatures than normal. Europeans have documented that a sauna, at least temporarily, increases immunity. Take one whenever possible, 2–3 times weekly is ideal.

Take supplements: A host of nutrients can help repair some of the damage that improper detoxification causes. Vitamin B_{12}, for example, helps rebuild cells in the lungs and Vitamin B_3 opens cells that nicotine has damaged. Take a good multi-vitamin that has mineral supplements.

Massage: A massage can be conducted on body-specific areas like the liver or kidneys that react positively to stimulation. Kidneys and liver are key organs in the elimination of toxins in the detoxification process. If you have a medical condition, seek advice from a physician before treating yourself, some oils can interfere with medical conditions including epilepsy and diabetes. Skin reflects the health of the entire body as the circulation system ends up depositing the toxins in the skin cells.

RECAP

➥ A healthy post-detox lifestyle also includes following a daily routine to rejuvenate inside and out by engaging in activities that are relaxing as well as stimulating.

▶▶

- One of the prime causes of a toxic body is diet.
- A regular regimen of exercise such as yoga, meditation, aromatherapy, therapeutic massage and a quiet period for introspection, are all integral steps for achieving lasting health and wellness.

SECTION VII

38

KNOW YOUR TOXINS

There are thousands of toxins spread around us, in the environment, within our bodies and in the products that we use, and it is not possible for us to know about all of them or even avoid all of them. However, it is possible to identify the toxins that we come across frequently, and once we know them, it becomes easier to avoid them.

Toxins on your dining table

Food adulteration is one of the major worries today as more toxins enter the body through food than through any other method. Most of these adulterants do not cause death, but lead to disastrous results in the long run. Most of the toxins are contained in the chemicals that are used in food to enhance its flavour, colour or increase its shelf life.

According to a recent study, Indians have the highest levels of pesticide residues in their bodies. There is poison in our food, a surfeit of toxins on our tables. Mull over these facts: Unbelievable though it seems, the meat that reaches your table most probably contains bleaching powder, which is commonly used to delay the process of dehydration in meat after the slaughter. When eaten, this dish could lead to vomiting and diarrhoea. High levels of toxic metals like lead, nickel, cadmium and chromium present in fruits and vegetables as well as cereals are consumed in each meal. A high level of chromium consumption can lead to damaged kidneys.

The sweetness of sugar hides in it the chalk powder that has been added to increase the quantity, the vinegar you use to enhance the taste of the dish may contain mineral acid that can be damaging to your body cells, the *laddoos* and *barfis* you distribute to celebrate a good news may be the harbinger of cancer since they contain lethal colouring agents. The cooking oil carries the oil of Argemone Mexicana, which contains an alkaloid called sanguinarine, which is highly toxic in nature and can cause nerve damage and paralysis. Even reputed brands have been found to resort to adulteration. In fact, a study conducted by National Dairy Development Board (NDDB) found that almost 90 per cent of available cooking oil in the market was adulterated with toxic metals like nickel and lead.

A few years back there were many cases of dropsy, paralysis and nerve debility reported in the eastern parts of the country. This happened due to the adulteration of edible pulses. Ice creams of inferior quality contain various degrees of bacteria, which can cause gastro-intestinal problems. Milk has been found to contain starch, caustic soda, urea, hydrogen peroxide and formalin. In fact, milk is the most adulterated product available for consumption. Vegetables and fruits are subjected to heavy doses of pesticides and fungicides and carry enough residual poison to harm both body and brain. They have been found to contain heavy metals like copper, lead and cadmium. Lead toxicity can lead to kidney failure and high blood pressure.

Condiments that are adulterated would cover an entire chapter; such is the ruthlessness of unscrupulous traders. A known carcinogenic element like metanil yellow is added to turmeric powder to give it a bright yellow tinge. Red chilli powder is made redder by adding Sudan I. These dyes are dangerous, but they are used indiscriminately to confound the consumer. The list is endless.

Although it may not be possible to identify or avoid all the adulterants, the common ones can be avoided. One thumb rule you can follow is to avoid all kinds of preservatives as well as artificially-coloured and flavoured foods.

Unless you grow all your food in your own garden and prepare all your meals from scratch, it's almost impossible to eat food without preservatives added by manufacturers during processing. Without such preservatives, bread would get mouldy, and salad oil would go rancid before it can be used. Food law says preservatives must be listed by their common or usual names on ingredient labels of all foods that contain them. You'll see calcium propionate on most bread labels, di-sodium EDTA on canned kidney beans, just to name a few. Even snack foods – dried fruit, potato chips, etc. contain sulphur-based preservatives. Manufacturers add preservatives mostly to prevent spoilage during the time it takes to transport foods over long distances to stores and then to our kitchens.

Preservatives serve as either anti-microbials or antioxidants – or both. As anti-microbials, they prevent the growth of moulds, yeasts and bacteria. As antioxidants, they keep foods from becoming rancid, browning or developing black spots. Antioxidants suppress the reaction that occurs when foods combine with oxygen in the presence of light, heat and some metals. Antioxidants also minimise the damage to some essential amino acids – the building blocks of proteins – and the loss of some vitamins.

Food additives are used to:

Maintain consistency or texture: To sustain smoothness or prevent the food from separating, caking or clumping.

Improve or retain nutritional value: Enrichment replaces nutrients lost in processing – this occurs with grains, as some vitamins and minerals are lost in the milling process. Fortification adds a nutrient that wasn't there before and may be lacking in many people's diets. Iodised salt is an example. This has proven useful in preventing goitre, a thyroid disease caused by the deficiency in iodine. Enriched and fortified foods are labelled as such.

Delay spoilage

Enhance flavour, texture, or colour

Preservatives are centuries old. Since ancient times, salt has been used to cure meats and fish, and sugar has been added to fruits to preserve them. Herbs, spices and vinegar have also served as preservatives. Natural additives are not harmful. It is only the chemical and synthetic ones which may cause toxic effect.

Some uses and examples of food additives are:

Anti-Oxidants: Prevent spoilage, flavour changes and loss of colour caused by exposure to air. Vitamin C and Vitamin E are used as antioxidants. E.g. ascorbic acid in butter.

Emulsifiers: Used to keep water and oil mixed together. Lecithin is one example used in margarine, baked goods and ice cream. Mono- and di-glycerides are another kind of emulsifiers found in similar foods and peanut butter. Polysorbate 60 and 80 are used in coffee lighteners and artificial whipped cream.

Thickening Agents: Absorb water in foods and keep the mixture of oil, water, acids and solids blended properly. Alginate is derived from seaweed and is used to maintain the texture in ice cream, cheese and yoghurt. Casein, a milk protein, is used in ice cream, sherbet and coffee creamers.

Colours: Make food more colourful; two examples are tartrazine and sunset yellow.

Flavour Enhancers: Bring out flavours in food; a well-known one is monosodium glutamate (MSG).

Anti-Caking Agents: Stop powdery foods from forming lumps, as in salt.

Nitrates: Act as a preservative in many foods but may be added to foods, such as pork, to give a pink colour.

These substances can sometimes adversely affect people who suffer from allergic conditions like asthma, hay fever, urticaria, etc. A few additives and preservatives can also affect non-allergic people. Some of these substances cause more reactions than others. For example, reactions to sulphur dioxide and sodium benzoate occur more commonly in asthmatics than reactions to the colorant tartrazine.

The reactions to food additives depend on the type of preservative or additive ingested. These may include vomiting, rashes, hives, a tight chest, headaches, worsening of eczema and many other symptoms.

Sulphur dioxide and sodium benzoate often cause 'tight chests' in individuals who have asthma. Many people also complain of a scratchy feeling at the back of their throats. Although these are the common reactions, others, such as rashes, may also occur. Sulphur dioxide may be labelled as sodium metabisulphite, potassium metabisulphite, sodium or potassium bisulphite or sulphite.

Some foods that may contain sulphur dioxide are:

Some fruit juices
Concentrated soft drinks
Dried fruit
Wine, beer
Some sauces
Pickles.

Some foods that may contain sodium benzoate include:

Fruit juices
Soft drinks
Foods with fruit

Flavour Enhancers: The most famous of these is monosodium glutamate, commonly called MSG. Eating foods with this additive may result in tight chests in asthmatics. This reaction may occur immediately or 6–12 hours later. A condition called 'Chinese Restaurant Syndrome' may occur in any individual. This reaction can occur about 20 minutes after a food containing MSG is eaten on an empty stomach. Typical symptoms include headache, a burning sensation along the back of the neck, chest tightness or pain, nausea, sweating and a sensation of facial pressure. 'Pins and needles' or tingling may be experienced in the limbs or face and head. It is not a common condition.

Some foods that may contain MSG are: oriental food, packet soups, sauces, soya sauce, seasoning. MSG is also thought to occur naturally in mushrooms and tomatoes.

Antioxidants: These are substances that prevent oily foods from becoming rancid. Some individuals complain of reactions to butylated hydroxyanisole (BHA) or butylated hydroxytoluene (BHT). Fortunately, reactions to these substances are not common. Reactions include rashes, hives, and occasionally 'tight' chests.

Colorants: Colorants may be natural or synthetic. Reactions, although not common, can occur to both types. The best-known colorant is tartrazine. Tartrazine is an azo dye, so if you react to this colorant, you should avoid all of the azo dyes. Although many people are concerned that they may be affected by colorants, not many individuals are in fact affected. Not all asthmatics need to avoid tartrazine. Whether tartrazine or other colorants can result in hyperactivity in children is still controversial.

Some common food adulterants

Food	Adulterant	Detection
Cumin seed	Dyed seeds of grass	The easiest way to detect the adulteration is to press a few seeds between the fingers. The dyed seeds would leave stain on the fingers.
Cinnamon	Dyed barks	Put a few pieces in a glass of water. If the colour runs, the cinnamon is adulterated.
Coffee seeds	Roasted bread crumbs, powdered date seeds	Drop a spoon of coffee seeds in a glass of water. The adulterated stuff will settle in the bottom while the genuine coffee seeds will float on top.

Black peppercorns	Papaya seeds	Drop the seeds in a glass of water. The papaya seeds will float on top while the genuine peppercorns will settle at the bottom.
Asafoetida	Sand, gum	Pure asafoetida blends with water to leave a whitish mixture. When burnt, it burns vigorously. Adulterated asafoetida turns the colour of water to light yellow.
Ghee/butter	Vanaspati/starch	To melted ghee/ butter add equal quantity of hydrochloric acid and shake. If the layer of acid turns pink, the ghee is adulterated.
Red chilli powder	Wood particles, red dye	Stir a spoon of red chilli powder in a glass of water. The wood particles will float. If the water turns red, it indicates that red dye has been added to the powder.

Sugar	Metal particles, white sand, chalk powder	The metal particles can be detected by using a magnet. Other adulterants will float on top when sugar is mixed in a glass of water.
Tea	Dyed used tea leaves, Wood shavings and iron particles	Spread some tea leaves on a blotting paper and leave for a while. If the tea leaves stains, the tea has been adulterated with used tea leaves. To detect iron particles, use a magnet. To detect the wood shavings, mix the tea leaves in water and the shavings will float up.

Some foods that may contain colorants include:
Fruit juices
Soft drinks
Sweets
Desserts
Toppings
Syrups
Cooking oils
Sauces
Pickles

Sweeteners: The artificial sweetener aspartame may cause rashes or hives in sensitive individuals. This sweetener is added to many 'low calorie' foods.

Salicylates: Acetyl salicylic acid found in aspirin may result in a 'tight' chest or hives in some asthmatics. A different form of salicylic acid can be found in a variety of spices and foods. Some health professionals believe that this form can result in many side effects, including hyperactivity in children. However, this is still controversial.

Toxins on your dressing table

This is the age of youth and beauty. The race is on, and the winner is the one who is youthful and good-looking. Appearance matters more than other things, and people are going all out to achieve a smooth skin, wrinkle-less face and sculpted bodies. Cosmetics to cover up blemishes, topical ointments to combat pimples, and collagen and botox injections to fight wrinkle – all kinds of remedies are up for grabs. People are mostly unaware or ignore the side effects that can be caused by the cosmetic products. Many skin-care products actually damage the skin barrier and clog detoxification pores, leading to a host of allergic conditions and other skin problems.

Many personal-care products like deodorants, aftershave lotions and cosmetics that are used by most of us contain chemicals that have been linked to breast cancer and birth defects. Some of these chemicals – including phthalates, acrylamide, formaldehyde and ethylene oxide – are listed by some American states as carcinogens.

According to a report by the Environmental Working Group (EWG), an astonishing one-third of all cosmetic products contain one or more ingredients such as coal tar, formaldehyde and lead acetate, all potentially linked to cancer. They found that 71 hair-dye products contained ingredients derived from carcinogenic coal tar. 55 per cent of all products assessed contained penetration enhancers – ingredients that can increase a product's penetration through the skin and into the blood stream, increasing consumers' exposures to other ingredients as well, the report says. And this is in USA, where the rules are much more stringent than in our country.

The skin is made up of two distinct layers, the epidermis and beneath it, the dermis. The outermost level of the epidermis, called the stratum corneum (SC), is most vulnerable to allergy and sensitivity. The SC is a network of cells on the surface of the skin that provides immediate protection from the outside world and helps restrict the loss of water. The SC requires three main types of lipids (fats) to form a healthy cutaneous barrier – ceramides (such as alpha-hydroxy and omega-hydroxy acids), cholesterol and polyunsaturated fatty acids (essential fatty acids).

When the lipids are tightly packed into the spaces between the SC cells, potentially harmful substances that touch the skin are unable to squeeze their way through the skin surface and enter the body. On the other hand, when there are disruptions in the number and compactness of the intercellular lipids, the skin barrier becomes permeable.

The exposed surface of the skin is constantly losing water due to environmental factors such as sun, wind and chemicals, to name a few. When the body is dehydrated, circulation to the base of the outer skin may be shut down as an emergency measure, so that water is not lost through evaporation from the skin's surface. Chronic dehydration shows in the face as wrinkles, lines and furrows.

There are numerous skin-care products that claim to keep the skin supple and youthful. What many of us don't realise is that some of these products contain ingredients that have been clinically proven to damage the skin barrier. Some of these are:

Sodium lauryl sulfate (SLS, also known as sodium laureth or lauryl sulfate) is a highly-irritating chemical cleanser that is found in many shampoos, conditioners, body washes and other skin-care products. It alters the nuclei in epidermal cells and also disturbs the SC lipids just beneath the skin surface. Discontinuing use of SLS-containing products is the only way to avoid the permeability caused by this chemical.

Acetone, another well-known irritant, is the main ingredient in nail-polish remover. In fact, these two chemicals are routinely used in lab experiments to induce skin permeability.

Retinoids and Retinoic Acid (Vitamin A) are popular in skin products advertised by cosmetic companies as components that decrease wrinkling, brown spots and acne. But anyone who has used products such as Retin-A knows about the side effects: dry skin, peeling and photo-sensitivity (adverse reactions to the sun). These effects are due to skin permeability induced by vitamin A. Several studies have found that retinoic acid loosens the cohesion of cells and lipids in the skin. While this process provides for greater elasticity and smoothness to the skin, it also causes barrier dysfunction, increased skin water loss and scaling.

Alkanes (Paraffin) are by-products of petroleum manufacturing, commonly used as the base of many topical lotions, cosmetics and hair-care products. Alkanes act like plastic bags when applied to the skin – they form a sealed film of grease on the skin barrier, impeding the absorption of oxygen from the air and blocking the elimination of wastes from within the body.

Continuous use of skin-care products containing alkanes and other saturated fats contributes to the development of allergy and sensitivity. The inability to eliminate wastes allows for toxins to accumulate in the subcutaneous connective and fatty tissue. Over time, this leads to lymphatic stress. When the detoxification pathways – lymph, skin, liver and other organs – are overloaded with toxins, the immune system will tend to overreact because it is overwhelmed with dangerous antigens. Allergic reactions are just one of the many symptoms of a hyperactive immune system caused by toxic overload.

Toxins in your washroom

We happily lather up all the soaps and detergents that are marketed by big companies with great gloss. A few facts about them could definitely help us in remaining healthier.

Soaps and detergents

Strip skin's precious moisture shield
Reduce body's immune barrier
Leave skin malnourished
Accelerate ageing

So, using less of them would definitely cut down on the harmful effects. Our body's biggest organ, the skin, is our most important immune defence barrier, as well as the largest organ for eliminating waste. Commercial products with harmful petroleum ingredients can clog your pores, making it easier for the germs to get trapped in and more difficult for the toxins to be excreted from your body.

Alcohol and solvents (propylene glycol)

Damage immune barrier
Deplete Moisture

Dissolve proteins
Encourage bacteria and parasite growth
Accelerate ageing

Every day we use products that we think are safe; but the truth is that products are not always safe, and manufacturers don't reveal all of it to us. There are as many as 25,000 chemicals that are put to use but have not been tested for long-term toxic effects. Each day, we might be exposed to over 200 different chemicals, many of which are suspected of causing cancer or affecting the hormones. Laboratory tests conclude that several ingredients in shampoos, dyes and other personal-care products could disturb the balance of hormones that control reproduction and development.

A good way to avoid the toxic chemicals is to begin reading the fine print about the ingredients that go into the manufacture of the products. Here are some hazardous ingredients that you would do well to avoid.

Some toxic ingredients

Alcohol, Isopropyl (SD-40): This is a very drying and irritating solvent and dehydrating agent that strips your skin's moisture and natural immune barrier, making you more vulnerable to bacteria, moulds and viruses. It is made from propylene, a petroleum derivative and is found in many skin and hair products, fragrance, antibacterial hand washes as well as shellac and antifreeze.

It can act as a 'transporter' and speed up the penetration of other harmful chemicals into the skin. It may encourage brown spots and premature ageing of skin. Researchers have found that it can cause headaches, flushing, dizziness, mental depression, nausea, vomiting, narcosis, anaesthesia and coma. Fatal ingested dose is one ounce or less.

Mineral Oil: Used widely, mineral oil is a petroleum by-product that coats the skin like plastic, clogging the pores. It also interferes with skin's ability to eliminate toxins, promoting acne and other disorders. It can slow down skin function and cell development, resulting in premature ageing. Here is a shocker – baby oil is 100 per cent mineral oil.

Colour Pigments: Synthetic colours made from coal tar, containing heavy metal salts that deposit toxins onto the skin, causing skin sensitivity and irritation. Absorption of certain colours can cause depletion of oxygen in the body and death. Tests on animals have shown almost all of them to be carcinogenic.

Perfumes: Although we use different kinds of perfumes, we remain blissfully unaware of the synthetic ingredients that go into them. Some of them can indicate the presence of up to 4,000 separate ingredients, a few of them toxic or carcinogenic. Scientists have found some of the fragrances to give rise to symptoms like headaches, dizziness, allergic rashes, skin discoloration, violent coughing and vomiting, and skin irritation. Clinical observation has proved that fragrances can affect the central nervous system, causing depression, hyperactivity, irritability and other behavioural changes.

Diethanolamine (DEA), Monoethanolamine (MEA) and triethanolamine (TEA): These contain hormone-disrupting chemicals that can form cancer-causing nitrates and nitrosamines in the body. The use of these chemicals has already been banned in Europe due to known carcinogenic effects. In the United States they are still used in products such as shampoos, shaving creams and bubble baths.

According to Dr Samuel Epstein, Professor of Environmental Health at the University of Illinois, the repeated skin applications of DEA-based detergents resulted in a major increase in the incidence of liver and kidney cancer. In children it can cause graver risk.

DMDM Hydantoin and Urea (Imidazolidinyl): These are just two of the many preservatives that often release formaldehyde, which may cause joint pain, skin reactions, allergies, depression, headaches, chest pains, ear infections, chronic fatigue, dizziness and loss of sleep. Exposure may also irritate the respiratory system, trigger heart palpitations or asthma, and aggravate coughs and colds. Other possible side effects include weakening the immune system and cancer.

Sodium Lauryl Sulfate (SLS) and Sodium Laureth Sulfate (SLES): Detergents and surfactants that pose serious health threats. Used in car washes, garage floor cleaners and engine degreasers. These two chemicals find use in almost 90 per cent of personal-care products that foam. Tests on animals exposed to SLS have shown them to experience eye damage, depression, laboured breathing, diarrhoea, severe skin irritation and even death. SLS may also damage the skin's immune system by causing layers to separate and inflame. When combined with other chemicals, SLS can be transformed into nitrosamines, a potent carcinogen. SLS can be retained in the body for up to five days, during which time, it may enter and leave residual deposits in the heart, liver, the lungs and the brain.

Polyethylene Glycol (PEG): A potential carcinogenic petroleum ingredient that can alter and reduce the skin's natural moisture factor. Besides making the user more vulnerable to bacteria, it can accelerate ageing. The chemical is used in cleansers to dissolve oil and grease. It adjusts the melting point and thickens products.

Propylene Glycol (PG) and Butylene Glycol: Gaseous

hydrocarbons that in a liquid state act as 'surfactant' (wetting agents and solvents). They easily penetrate the skin and can weaken protein and cellular structure. Chew on this: PG is strong enough to remove barnacles from boats. It is used for making extracts from herbs. Experts consider PG so toxic that they recommend factory workers to wear protective gloves, clothing and goggles and to dispose of any PG solutions by burying them in the ground. Because PG penetrates the skin so quickly, experts warn against skin contact to prevent consequences such as brain, liver and kidney abnormalities. But there isn't even a warning label on products such as stick deodorants, where the concentration is greater than in most industrial applications.

Triclosan: A deadly synthetic antibacterial ingredient with a chemical structure similar to Agent Orange. Scientists catalogue it as a pesticide, giving it high scores as a risk to both human health and the environment. It is classified as a chlorophenol, a class of chemicals suspected of causing cancer in humans. Its manufacturing process may produce dioxin, a powerful hormone-disrupting chemical with toxic effects measured in the parts per trillion; that is only one drop in 300 Olympic-size swimming pools! Hormone disruptors pose enormous long-term chronic health risks by interfering with the way hormones perform, such as changing genetic material, decreasing fertility and sexual function, and fostering birth defects. It can temporarily deactivate sensory nerve endings, so contact with it often causes little or no pain. Internally, it can lead to cold sweats, circulatory collapse and convulsions. Stored in body fat, it can accumulate to toxic levels, damaging the liver, kidneys and lungs, and can cause paralysis, suppression of immune function, brain haemorrhages and heart problems. Tufts University School of Medicine says that triclosan is capable of forcing the emergence of 'super bugs' that it cannot kill. Its widespread use in popular antibacterial cleansers, toothpastes and household products may have nightmarish implications for our future.

These are just a few of the known chemicals that are in circulation. A complete list could confound consumers who have never given a thought to the kind of ingredients that go into the production of the vast range or products that are commonly used in day-to-day living. Stricter governmental controls and regulations are the only methods to control the menace.

Toxins in your water

Apart from the umpteen number of pollutants, the very chemical used to cleanse water could be toxic in nature. For decades we have believed that chlorination of water is the best way to purify it, but recent studies by scientists have found that chlorination of water could lead to several kinds of cancers in the long run.

According to a study published in the *Journal of the National Cancer Institute*, long-term drinking of chlorinated water appears to increase a person's risk of developing bladder cancer by as much as 80 per cent. Scientists do not believe that chlorine itself causes problems but suspect that the actual cause of the bladder cancers is a group of chemicals that form as a result of reactions between chlorine and natural substances and pollutants in water such as organic matters which could be leaves and twigs as well. According to US Council of Environmental Quality, cancer risk among people drinking chlorinated water is 93 per cent higher than among those whose water does not contain chlorine. While it prevented epidemics of one disease, it was creating those of another.

In certain parts of the country, the water contains high levels of fluoride. Fluoride is a known poison, classified as toxic to extremely toxic by the National Library of Medicine, USA. It fights tooth decay topically by poisoning the bacteria that cause the decay. It is more likely to poison the vital organs also, when used indiscriminately.

Metals such as aluminium are also hazardous to health. Scientists believe that aluminium ingested over a period of time could lead to Alzheimer's disease.

Toxins in your dental filling

While getting our dental cavities filled, most of us never give a thought to the mix that goes into the tooth as a filling. In a shocking revelation, scientists revealed that the mercury that goes into the amalgam could lead to several health problems. The mercury could get deposited in the liver and cause heavy metal toxicity.

A typical amalgam filling contains about 1,000mg of mercury. Researchers say that every time the filling is exposed to pressure from chewing, mercury vapours are released in the body, whereby heavy metal accumulates in the liver and other organs.

Most of us harbour in our bodies tiny pieces of metal, like mercury (from your fillings) or lead, or even iron. They are like time bombs, waiting to cause trouble. Although they are too minute to be detected by naked eyes, these are tiny pieces of metal are quite toxic in nature. They can cause heart disease and cancer. These pieces of metal can be so small that they can easily get embedded inside some tissue or organ of the body. Especially mercury has been known to get lodged in the liver. Sometimes, the tissue or organ tries to protect itself from this dangerous toxic metal by growing more tissue around the toxic metal, much like the clam secreting nacre around a foreign body. The proliferation of body cells around the heavy metal forms a lump, over a period of time, which could cause cancer.

Mercury from fillings in pregnant women has been shown to cause mercury accumulation in the brain, kidneys and liver of human foetuses. Studies have shown that mercury can be passed to infants via breast milk.

You could detoxify the body of excess mercury, to a certain extent, by oral chelation. Natural herbs such as garlic and cilantro have been found helpful in the detoxification of mercury. Start eating garlic regularly to enhance sulphur levels in the body. 2–3 cloves a day is quite adequate, but make sure you crush it to release its active ingredients. Cilantro helps to mobilise mercury out of the tissue, so it can be excreted easily. In fact, herbs are a potent method of detoxification. Gentle, natural laxatives such as cascara sagrada soften caked food, making it easier to eliminate. Black walnut hulls also help do this, as well as having the extra advantage of being an anti-parasitic. Licorice root may help the liver detoxify. Marshmallow and shave grass are classified as lithotriptics by herbalists, which mean that they dissolve, and discharge urinary and gallbladder stones.

39

ASSESS YOUR TOXIN LEVEL

It helps to know where one stands as far as health and well-being are concerned. In the following section are some questionnaires, which will serve as health pointers and help you assess your health level – both physical and emotional.

A sound mind

The following questionnaire has been designed by the International Medical Association to assess the mental health of an adult.

Are you always worrying?

Are you unable to concentrate because of unrecognised reasons?

Are you continually unhappy without a justified cause?

Do you lose your temper easily and often?

Are you troubled by regular insomnia?

Do you have wide fluctuations in mood from depression to elation and back to depression, incapacitating you for work?

Do you continually dislike being with people?

Are you upset if the routine of your life is disturbed?

Do your children constantly get on your nerves?

Are you 'browned off' and constantly bitter?

Are you always right and the other person always wrong?

Are you afraid without real cause?

Do you have numerous aches and pains for which no doctor can find a physical cause?

Do you often belittle people and make fun of them or criticise them behind their backs?

Do you always speak in a raised and offensive tone?

Score: give yourself one mark for each 'yes'.

Verdict: Positive answers to more than 12 questions are warning signals of poor mental health. You require professional help if a definite 'yes' occurs for each of the above questions.

Toxic anger

There are three factors that determine the toxicity of anger – the frequency, intensity and duration of a flare-up. Here is a quiz designed to enlighten you on your anger-toxicity level. To find honest answers consult someone who is close to you and recognises the range of your anger.

1. On an average, what is the frequency of angry flare-ups in one week?

Not a single one (b) 1–3 times (c) More than 3 times (d)About 2–3 times each day (e) About 4–5 times each day (f) More than 5 times each day

2. How long does your flare-up generally last?

Less than 5 minutes (b) About 7–10 minutes (c) less than ½ hour (d) Less than 1 hour (e) ½– 1 day (f) More than 1 day

3. How intense is your anger? On a scale of 1–10 mark your level of intensity

Score: For the first question if your answer ranges from (a) to (c), give yourself 1 mark and if the answer is (d) or (e) give yourself 2 marks and for (f) you get 3 marks.

For the second question give yourself 1 mark if the answer is (a) or (b), 2 marks for (c) and (d), and 3 marks for (e) and (f).

In case of the third question give yourself 1 mark if you range somewhere between 1 and 3, 2 marks if the range is between 4–6, and 3 marks for above 6.

Verdict: While calculating the damaging effects of anger, the three factors – frequency, intensity and duration have to be taken into account. Although a person may have infrequent eruptions of anger, if the intensity or duration is high, it is a cause for concern. Similarly, more frequent outburst with low intensity can be equally damaging. The idea is to evaluate the emotion in totality. Experts divide the angry into three distinct categories. 'The volcanoes' are those who have high-frequency and high-intensity outburst. The sleeping lions are those who suffer from high-intensity and long-duration eruptions, and lastly, the slow burners who have high-frequency and long-duration flare-ups.

If you have scored under 4, you have an excellent grip on your anger, and it is not likely to have negative effects on you or your family and friends. It is human to harbour a bit of anger. Be mature in dealing with issues and keep a lid over your temper. In the long run you will emerge a winner.

If you've scored between 5–7, your angry outbursts could have a negative impact on your relationships and health. While anger is difficult to control, the effort to do so is always fruitful. Success kisses those who can tame the emotions. Your level of outburst is not lethal enough to be written off because this level can be controlled through meditation and other techniques.

If you've scored anything above 7, you are in a danger zone. It is toxic anger for sure. Anger at this level can reduce your ability as a nurturing parent, and cause marital disharmony and even shorten life expectancy. People with high anger levels often suffer social ostracism, and success eludes them. Besides, the health problems that accompany toxic anger make it imperative for you to examine your emotional control. Since it is at a high level, it may not be possible for you to find success in dealing with your anger alone. It may be wiser to seek expert help.

40

LIFESTYLE EVALUATION

Here are some questions to help you evaluate your lifestyle. They can serve as guides to a healthier and toxin-free existence.

Diet evaluation log

How many times do you eat at fast-food joints in a week?

Frequency:	0–1	2–4	5–7	8–10	more than 10
Points:	1	2	3	4	5

Number of soft drinks consumed per week

Frequency:	0–1	3–5	6–8	9–11	12 or more
Points:	1	2	3	4	5

Number of servings consumed of green, leafy vegetables, per week

Frequency:	15+	11–14	8–10	5–7	less than 4
Points:	1	2	3	4	5

Number of non-vegetarian meals eaten per week

Frequency:	0–3	4–7	8–10	11–13	14 or more
Points:	1	2	3	4	5

Number of teaspoons of sugar added to tea/coffee per week

Frequency:	0–1	2–3	4–5	6–7	8 or more
Points:	1	2	3	4	5

Cups of tea/coffee consumed per day

Frequency:	0–1	2–3	4–5	6–7	8 or more
Points:	1	2	3	4	5

Slices of whole grain bread eaten per week

Frequency:	14 or more	12–14	9–11	6–8	less than 5
Points:	1	2	3	4	5

Number of sweet desserts consumed per week

Frequency:	0–3	4–6	7–10	11–14	15 or more
Points:	1	2	3	4	5

Number of meals or snacks with milk or low-fat cheese, per week

Frequency:	9 or more	7–8	5–6	3–4	0–2
Points:	1	2	3	4	5

Number of days per week when three balanced meals are not eaten.

Frequency	0–1	2	3	4	5 or more
Points	1	2	3	4	5

Your Score:

Less than 15: Congrats! Your diet is perfect. Maintaining it at this level will definitely keep your body fit and toxin free.

15 to 20: You are doing quite well. Keep it up! An honest look at the toxic elements that can be cut out will help you score better.

20 to 30: You tend to let yourself go at times. Your score is not too bad, but you would do better by keeping toxic food out of reach.

30 to 40: You have a poor diet, which could lead to several problems in the long run. Work your way towards a lower score for optimum health.

41 or more: You have a problem here. A complete revamp of your dietary element is required, if you are keen on living a long and healthy life.

Activity evaluation log

1. Do you usually walk upstairs or take the lift?

Walk	Take the lift
A	B

2. Do you walk at least a part of the way to work or do you rely on some vehicle?

Walk	Use a vehicle
A	B

3. Do you have a regular exercise programme?

Yes	No
A	B

4. Is your resting pulse above 80 beats per minute?

No	Yes
A	B

5. Do you have high blood pressure?

No	Yes
A	B

6. Are you overweight?

No	Yes
A	B

7. Are you diabetic or do you have a tendency to blood-sugar problems?

No	Yes
A	B

8. Do you feel tired and run-down quite often?

No	Yes
A	B

9. Has your body shape changed so that funny bulges are popping out all over?

No	Yes
A	B

10. Do you get out of breath while walking up a flight of stairs?

No	Yes
A	B

11. Do you smoke?

No	Yes
A	B

12. Do you have chest pain, recurrent headaches or ringing of your ears?

No	Yes
A	B

13. Does high altitude (above 5000 ft.) cause shortness of breath?

No	Yes
A	B

14. Can you fit into the jeans you bought five years back?

No	Yes
A	B

Your Score:

Give yourself 1 mark for each A and 0 for each B.

Verdict:

12 to 14: You have an excellent activity record. Your heart must be singing with glee. Keep up the good job.

10 to 11: Although your score is quite good, you can do better by incorporating a little more activity in your everyday life.

08 to 09: Your activities can be termed as average. There is need for more activity in your daily schedule. Try introducing an extra ten-minute regimen in the routine.

06 to 07: Poor show, needs improvement. Sluggish lifestyle leads to much more problems than one can imagine. Begin by introducing a regimen of 10–15 minutes and work your way to about 20 minute activity, at least three times a week.

05 or less: There is no doubt about the fact that your lifestyle is totally sedentary. You need to shed inactivity and walk your way to health. Activate yourself immediately!

Leisure evaluation log

1. Do you have at least half an hour of quiet time to yourself each day?

Yes	No
A	B

2. Are you always running short of time and snapping at everyone?

No	Yes
A	B

3. Do you feel you haven't achieved all you wanted to, at the end of the day?

No	Yes
A	B

4. Do most days give you a feeling of being stressed?
    No — Yes
    A — B
5. Do you suffer from stress-elevated blood pressure?
    No — Yes
    A — B
6. Do you have great difficulty in enjoying a vacation?
    No — Yes
    A — B
7. Do you feel a week after an enjoyable vacation that it never happened?
    No — Yes
    A — B
8. Do you have time for conversation with the people whose company you enjoy?
    Yes — No
    A — B
9. When you have time for leisure, do you not know what to do with yourself?
    No — Yes
    A — B
10. Do you have a group of friends and family who support your leisure time needs?
    Yes — No
    A — B
11. Is your leisure time scheduled too tightly for your true enjoyment?
    No — Yes
    A — B

Your Score:
Give yourself 1 mark for each A and 0 for each B.

Verdict:

08 to 09: That's perfect! You understand the value of life and have taken care to keep some time aside for leisure. Leisure is important, both for the body as well as mind. Try to schedule some more time for yourself.

04 to 06: You are stingy with your 'me time'. Work on setting aside at least half an hour of your time for yourself.

02 to 03: Frankly speaking, your idea of leisure time is not too good. You must make an earnest effort to include more leisure time in your daily routine.

Less than 02: You just don't know the meaning of leisure. Perhaps you think leisure is a waste of time. Honestly, you need to re-examine where you are headed. Slow down and breathe easy! Work out some time for yourself, it will pay high dividend in the long run.

Workplace environment evaluation

1. Do enjoy going to work and look forward to spending the day at work?

Never	Sometimes	Frequently	Always
1	2	3	4

2. Do you feel happy with your job role and activities at work?

Never	Sometimes	Frequently	Always
1	2	3	4

3. Do you feel your working hours are too long and tiring?

Never	Sometimes	Frequently	Often
1	2	3	4

4. Do you experience passive smoking inside the office?

Quite a lot	Just a little	Very little	There is a separate smoke area
1	2	3	4

5. Does a noisy environment add to your stress level?

Always	Sometimes	Seldom	Never
1	2	3	4

6. Are you confined to your desk or do you get an opportunity to take breaks?

Never	Sometimes	Frequently	Very often
1	2	3	4

7. Is healthy interaction between the employees a regular feature?

Never	Sometimes	Quite often	Very often
1	2	3	4

8. Does the workplace provide enough recreational activities?

No such thing	Not adequate	Quite adequate	Plenty
1	2	3	4

9. Is there a system which examines the availability of comfort elements to the staff?

No such thing	Inadequate	Quite adequate	Very effective
1	2	3	4

10. Are you exposed to hazardous and toxic elements at work?

Significant exposure	Frequently	Occasionally	Never
1	2	3	4

Your Score:

36 to 40: Lucky You! Your workplace has excellent environment. You are unlikely to suffer from any of the problems related to toxic work environments like high stress levels and sleep-related problems.

30 to 35: Although it is not a perfect set-up, your work environment is good enough to promote efficient working conditions.

25 to 29: You are presently working in a place with moderate working environment. Maybe you could suggest a few alterations to create a better set up.

20 to 24: You are currently working in an unhealthy environment. It may be worthwhile to scout around for a job that provides healthier work environment.

Less than 20: Do you think you should stick around in the unhealthy environment of your work place? It is definitely time to make a move to a better job.

Intellectual stimulation evaluation log

1. Do you have activities, hobbies, interests or pastimes that challenge your level of intellect?

No	Infrequently	Frequently	Very frequent
1	2	3	4

2. Do you read books and magazines designed to provoke critical thinking?

No	Sometimes	Frequently	Routinely
1	2	3	4

3. Is reading an important activity of the day?

No	Sometimes	Frequently	Major activity
1	2	3	4

4. Do you take active interest in art, literature or music?

No	Sometimes	When I have a chance	Very interested
1	2	3	4

5. Are you involved in educating yourself in some new field?

No	Sometimes	Frequently	Very often
1	2	3	4

6. Do you visit a library, or subscribe to magazines and periodicals?

No	Subscribe to magazine	Go to library	Both
1	2	3	4

7. Do you have a circle of friends who stimulate you intellectually? How often do you meet up with them?

Rarely	Sometimes	Frequently	Very often
1	2	3	4

8. Do you watch informative stuff on the television?

Rarely	Sometimes	Frequently	Almost always
1	2	3	4

9. Have you kept yourself updated on the latest in computers and information technology?

Not really	A little bit	Quite a lot	Up to date
1	2	3	4

10. How politically and environmentally aware are you?

I don't care	Partly aware	Quite aware	Very aware
1	2	3	4

Your Score:

36 to 40: Your intellectual stimulation is excellent.

30 to 35: Your attempt at maintaining intellectual stimulation is commendable.

25 to 29: You are moderately informed but could do better with a little more effort.

20 to 24: Tsk! Tsk! Your intellect is crying for more stimulation.

Less than 20: There is an immediate need of intellectual element in your lifestyle.

Note: These are just a few sample formats; you could incorporate many such questionnaires to evaluate and work on altering your lifestyle.

EPILOGUE

Those who have reached the end of the book and managed to put in a sincere effort towards making even a slight change in their lifestyle should pat themselves for the good beginning they have made. A sincere start often augurs a complete overhaul of the body, mind and soul. And when the start has been made, the end cannot be too far away. While most of your friends are busy spending a fortune buying all kinds of cosmetics that flood the supermarket shelves, especially the ones that promise to retard ageing, you could attain a radiant complexion and youthful looks through detoxification. The truth is that the cosmetic effects are only skin deep. They can't retard ageing nor transform an ageing skin into glowing one.

When you begin to collect the compliments for your radiant skin, remember that detoxification is not a single-time ritual. Keep working on the emotions in a regular manner. It is most important to work on the toxic emotions because most often they are the accelerators of the ageing process. The resentment, hostility, regret, anger or grievances you carry in your heart causes far more damage than the little bits of toxins you ingest every day.

Healthy living comes through controlled lifestyle, and who would know that better than you!